How YOl
a Famou:
2019

Use the Newest Strategies in Social
Media and Digital Marketing and
Facebook Advertising to Explode
your Personal Brand and YouTube
Channel is 2019

Written by Leo Fitzpatrick

purposes only. All effort has been executed to present accurate, up to date, and reliable, complete information. No warranties of any kind are declared or implied. Readers acknowledge that the author is not engaging in the rendering of legal, financial, medical or professional advice. The content within this book has been derived from various sources. Please consult a licensed professional before attempting any techniques outlined in this book.

By reading this document, the reader agrees that under no circumstancesis the author responsible for any losses, direct or indirect, which are incurred as a result of the use of information contained within this document, including, but not limited to, —errors, omissions, or inaccuracies.

Table of Contents

YouTube Trends in 2019

People all over the world know what YouTube is. Although it started as a simple idea, no one expected it to explode in popularity as fast as it did. We just wrapped up 2018, and it's now time to look at the future. Since YouTube became so popular, people have been coming up with revolutionary strategies to share with the world and to attract more audiences.

Nowadays, we see some social media platforms shutting down because they don't have enough users to keep them running. But this has never been the case with YouTube. More and more people are creating their own channels to either educate, entertain, or boost their businesses through social media marketing. Millions of users have started building their careers through YouTube monetization. Because of this amazing new concept, even the most ordinary people can become famous.

In itself, YouTube is a huge trend. But within this

social media site, trends also happen, and if you want to stay on top, you should keep up. Despite it being hugely popular, a lot of people still don't know too much about YouTube itself. Because it's so easy to use, people don't even bother learning more about it. So before we dive into the ways you can explode your YouTube channel and become an internet sensation, we need to get down to the basics.

Changes to Expect in YouTube and Social Media Marketing This 2019

There are different reasons for wanting to create your own YouTube channel. You may want to learn how to become an expert video creator, to entertain audiences by showcasing your talents, to teach people new skills, to expand your brand, and so much more. Ensuring your success means that the first thing you need to do is to learn all that you can about this social media giant.

What's In Store for YouTube in 2019?

YouTube isn't just about the channels anymore. Now, we are more focused on the videos shared on YouTube and the audiences they're reaching. Whatever your reason is for wanting to become a YouTube sensation, the key is to find the right kinds of viewers to watch what you're sharing. One of the changes you may notice on YouTube is that it has gotten rid of channel suggestions and it now makes suggestions based on content that's similar to what you're most frequently engaging in.

This means that the AI behind YouTube is attempting to predict what the viewers are watching. It makes use of certain signals such as if you subscribe to the channel you're viewing or how often you watch a particular video. When it comes to social media marketing and getting famous on YouTube, it's important to understand your audiences so you can also understand the things that they want. In doing this, YouTube itself will start helping you promote your videos. To better understand YouTube, let's take a look at some of the biggest trends we will see in 2019:

- **Long-term strategies**

  A few years back, YouTube was only about publishing videos often. Back then, more than 60% of the views would occur on the first day after a video got published. But now, that percentage has come down to only about 28%. This means that you may have to wait for some time before you see your video become popular if it does at all. Because of this, it's important to think about your long-term strategies and how you will keep audiences interested in what you have to offer.

- **Audience retention**

  Audience retention doesn't just mean shares and likes. It's more of when a person keeps on watching a video or at least a part of it. In some cases, the audiences may also subscribe to the video as they're watching them over and over again. Ideally, one of the main indicators you would like to see is that about half of those who watch your videos stay on all the way to the end.

- **Crossovers**

Becoming a powerful presence on YouTube means that you may have to create a series of content that is related to one another. For instance, instead of publishing a really long video, you can turn it into a mini-series with multiple parts. You can also create several channels which cross over and relate to each other. No matter how you do it, you want your viewers to become engaged and keep on watching similar content which all comes from you.

- **Video translation**

There's now a huge growth coming from

different regions such as India and the Asia Pacific. One of the top channels on YouTube now happens to be a Hindi channel which mostly publishes Indian music videos. This is just one example of why there's a growing need to translate channels.

Translating videos is especially important for those who plan to create educational channels -anyone in the world can learn. For entertainment channels, the need for translation may vary depending on the channel's genre.

- **View your impressions versus click-through data**

If you want to improve the views of your channel, there are plenty of things you can do. There are several tools available such as YouTube analytics which can help you measure the improvement of your views. According to the experts, a click-through rate of 12% is already considered "good." But the more important thing is that your click-through rate should be higher than your competition.

There are other tools available online which you can use to split-test thumbnails as YouTube doesn't offer this feature yet. Such tools can also allow you to check your real-time analytics. As a matter of fact, if you have several thumbnails and you see that one of your videos is performing poorly, it would be best to change its thumbnail.

- **Storytelling**

Everyone loves stories no matter where they come from. Sometimes, even if you publish a long video, if it's about a really compelling story, viewers will watch it all the way to the end. And when you just use facts when telling your story, more people will be paying attention to them.

If you want your channel to be all about telling stories, make sure to show vulnerability and transparency. However, you shouldn't try too hard to tell the story. Rather, you should just let it come naturally so people will see it as more meaningful. For instance, if you have experienced struggles in your life, you may share them. These types of stories resonate with people, especially if they end in you overcoming those struggles and coming out victorious. Such stories can inspire people and encourage them to keep moving forward no matter how difficult life may get.

- **Ad-pods**

Ad-pods refers to a stack of two ad spots which viewers can skip and which are delivered as mid-roll and pre-roll ads back-to-back. The great thing about ad-pods is that they don't interrupt the viewers. Instead, these ads get sent at different spots throughout the video. These ad-pods may help advertisers acquire more engagement from audiences. Although it's not a "big thing" yet, it's sure to become a trending concept in 2019.

- **YouTube and television**

In the past, people only used their televisions to watch movies, TV shows, and commercials. But with the advent of Smart TVs, more and more people have begun using these devices to watch YouTube videos. This is another trend which shows the potential of YouTube and how important it will be in 2019 and in the years to come. It means that advertisers and video brands can make themselves more known through YouTube and targeting the viewers who watch a lot of YouTube videos on their television screens.

These days, a lot of people are using their

televisions to watch YouTube videos. This means that video brands or advertisers may want to launch their ad campaigns by targeting the viewers to watch a lot of YouTube videos on TV.

- **YouTube live**

When you broadcast live on YouTube, you can allow your audiences to participate actively via live chat. For instance, if you're promoting your brand through YouTube live, your customers can ask you questions right there and then about the services or products you're selling. This feature helps you provide efficient customer service. Furthermore, businesses can share their brand with real-time audiences who are always interested in watching live videos.

- **YouTube chatbots**

Incorporating chatbots into YouTube will make it possible to have automatic conversations with customers. This is why these chatbots are another important trend coming in 2019. For businesses, they can help reduce customer support and sales costs. These businesses can provide 24-hour support to their customers without having to be online that long too.

- **YouTube influencer platforms**

Right now, the different brands have collaborated with the creators of YouTube to either brand products or place ads as influencer platforms. These platforms are an excellent source for businesses to acquire sales through real-time clients.

- **Branded content**

One of the most impactful sources for attracting customers from the viewers is YouTube is native video advertising. Although it costs quite a bit to launch a video with content about your own brand, the results you would get from it would usually be more than what you're expecting.

- **360-degree video content**

A lot of 360-degree videos are getting published on YouTube. These types of videos are giving the viewers an immersive experience which is different from what they have seen in the past. A lot of brands who use video advertising are providing such videos to their viewers so they can explore their brand better.

- **Personalized videos**

These days, audiences prefer to watch personalized videos. Such videos have the aim of sharing a person's individualized experience with their audiences. They're exciting, compelling, and have become a huge topic in video and social media marketing.

- **New formats of video ads**

YouTube provides businesses an avenue to create video ads which will compel their audiences. There are now different types of formats for video ads such as overlay ads, non-skippable or skippable video ads, display ads, bumper ads, and more.

- **Vertical videos**

These types of videos have emerged because they are more suitable for mobile devices which is where a lot of videos are watched. Vertical videos are more comfortable and easier to watch on mobile devices giving the audiences a better experience.

Video Marketing Trends to Follow on YouTube

Nowadays, a lot of people all over the world spend most of their time holding on to their mobile devices. And most of them are watching videos on YouTube whenever they have the chance. This is exactly the reason why YouTube videos are becoming so popular. So if you want to become one of those famous YouTubers in 2019, you need to learn the current video marketing trends and keep up with them.

- **360-degree videos**

  Since these types of videos were introduced, they've shown everyone how interactive and unique they can be. Therefore, their utilization in social media marketing in 2019 will just keep on growing. 360-degree videos provide viewers with an amazing way to immerse themselves in the video you've shared. These videos are perfect for travel-centric businesses, real estate, promotions and events, car dealerships, and so much more.

- **Live Video**

  Because of the live video feature, businesses can grow and explode on

YouTube in 2019. As a matter of fact, reports have shown that the daily watch times for YouTube live and other live video feeds have grown significantly over the past year. When you use live video, your audiences will feel like you're interacting or speaking with them directly. And they have the choice to "converse" with you by asking real-time questions or typing comments. Live videos add an element of personalization to your videos which, in turn, encourages the viewers to stick around all the way until the end.

- **Virtual reality**

For a lot of companies, virtual reality is nothing but an emerging trend. But this year, it's expected to become more mainstream and accessible for different types of businesses. Experts believe that it's going to be so popular that by the year 2020, the economic effect of augmented and virtual reality may reach up to $29.5

billion!

- **Vlogging**

This type of social media marketing has become extremely popular on YouTube. What the vloggers do is film different parts of their daily lives no matter if they're exciting or mundane. These days, entrepreneurs and businesses have started creating their own vlogging videos as well. The main reason for this is that vlogging gives the audiences a peek into your real life so you can establish a better and stronger connection with your viewers. Vlogging is an excellent way to grow an audience for your business because it's extremely affordable. All you would need for this is a high-quality smartphone, a type of video editing app, and your own YouTube channel.

- **YouTube ads**

In the past, television was the best place

for businesses to play their ads since they can reach thousands of people by just broadcasting a single advertisement. But as we enter 2019, more and more companies will turn to YouTube for their advertising needs. YouTube ads are cheaper than television ads and they have the potential to reach more audiences. In fact, a study which was commissioned by Google showed that in an average week, more adults tune in to YouTube than prime time television via mobile phones alone. Because of this, companies will become more interested in getting their YouTube ads out there for a larger audience to see.

The Emerging Importance of YouTube in 2019

Whether you're a business owner, an entrepreneur or you're just interested in becoming a famous YouTuber, you may have already heard about the different types of marketing methodologies. While doing research, you will always come across information pertaining to the importance of social media marketing and now, this can be applied to YouTube in a huge way.

More and more people are gaining interest in earning money through YouTube. Even if you're not an entrepreneur, you may want to get in on the action too. Although those savvy influencers make it look easy, the fact is, not everyone will be able to accomplish this no matter how much they want it. For those lucky ones who have become famous YouTubers and are now making a lot of money because of their fame, they achieved this by creating a social media marketing campaign with a superior strategy. Such a campaign should:

- be cost-effective

- be well-researched

- provide instant feedback to the consumers

- increase the public reviews

- connect with others easily and keep them engaged

- provide superior customer service

- increase the awareness of your brand

As a social media platform, YouTube covers all of these points. Aside from that, YouTube already has almost 2 billion users who are actively viewing the videos published online. Right now, YouTube has surpassed the number of users of Gmail, making this social media site the most popular service online. Soon, we may see YouTube surpass Facebook which currently has more than 2 billion active users.

The great thing about YouTube is that it's not showing any signs of slowing down. One of the main reasons why people love using YouTube is that you don't have to pay a fee when you want to post any kind of video. As long as you follow the guidelines set by YouTube, you have the freedom to post content free of charge. Also, YouTube provides some great tools and features for marketing, analytics, and editing which are also free. Right now, there's no other type of social media or sharing site which offers the same things. Other cool features it has to offer are:

- Live streaming where you can engage with your viewers in real-time

- The ability to create and upload different types of videos to create memorable impressions

- The ability to create your own YouTube series to captivate your target audience

- The chance to earn from the videos you publish if you get enough views

- The ability to create how-to videos for your viewers and even include your website link in the video's description

You can also market yourself and your brand on YouTube in such a way that it will attract the "right type" of audiences. There are even services available which you can hire where you would pay people to watch, like, and share your videos. When done right, you might even see your published video cross that 100k mark in just a matter of months!

Chapter 1: All About YouTube

YouTube is a type of social media platform and online communications site that's open to the public. Upon registration, the site allows its users to upload their videos and have them available to other users for viewing. But you don't have to register to view videos. Anyone who visits the site has access to them. The videos available on YouTube range from amateur ones made by beginners to the more professional ones made by more skilled individuals. Basically, you can upload just about any type of video on YouTube. This means that you can also view any type of video on the site as well. There are countless videos on the site which are compelling, educational, entertaining, and unique.

What is YouTube?

At its very core, YouTube is a website for sharing videos. Google has owned this site since the year

2006 and since then, it has grown to become a behemoth of online videos. Each day, about a billion hours' worth of videos are viewed on the site. In terms of content, YouTube contains everything under the sun. From DIY tips to music videos and more, you will find anything that you'd like to see there. If you've already registered on YouTube, then you can start uploading your videos. Simply download the YouTube app on your smartphone and you can capture videos and upload them directly.

How to Use YouTube

This giant social media site was the very first large-scale sharing site for videos and it's available all over the world and in more than 50 different languages. Basically anybody who has an internet connection can register on YouTube and share their content. Whether you just want to share your story online or you want to do something to help your business, you can do this on YouTube. Since anyone can upload content, you have an incredible array of viewable content.

After creating an account on the site, you can start uploading videos, creating playlists, getting personalized results, and commenting on other users' videos. The more you use the site, the more it will be able to learn about your preferences. For instance, you keep on watching videos about learning how to cook Mediterranean dishes. The next time you log into your account, the site will automatically suggest more videos about learning how to cook Mediterranean dishes. This is a special feature of YouTube which personalizes what it shows to its users to give them a more relevant experience. But you also have the option to not have YouTube save your preferences. To do this, simply watch videos on YouTube without signing in to your Google or YouTube account. When it comes to searching for videos on the site, there are different ways to do it:

- You can browse the videos through a keyword or a keyword phrase.

- You can search for videos in categories and topics.

- You can filter the results by popularity and date.

- You can view the rankings of videos in different categories.

- You can read about the trending topics found at the bottom of the category pages.

When you're watching a video on YouTube, you may notice that there's a section for comments right under it. Most of the videos on the site have this section where you can say what you want about what you just watched. However, some of the users may choose to disable this section so they won't receive any comments. Of course, you can only post your comments if you're logged on.

If you happen to discover a video that you really like and you want to share it with other people, there are different ways you can do this too such as emailing the video's link or embedding or sharing the URL of the video on your social media account. Just click on the "Share" button and you will see the different options for sharing the video with your family and friends. This sharing option is the main reason why a lot of videos on YouTube go viral. The sharing trend has become a worldwide phenomenon where millions of people get to watch a video and it gains that many views.

There is a wealth of videos just waiting to be discovered on YouTube and if you find those which you particularly enjoy, there are several ways for you to save them. You can create your own playlist of your favorite videos on YouTube allowing you to view them in a continuous stream. You can create different playlists then add the videos to them just by clicking on the "Add to" button. You also have the option to subscribe to the user's account, especially if you love all the videos that user uploads and you want to keep on watching them. This is another excellent way to save videos and watch them over and over again whenever you want to.

Apart from watching videos, you can also share your own videos for all the world to see. If you're itching to let the world know about your life, you can easily join the hundreds of thousands of people all over the world who are already uploading content each day. The good news is that the creators of YouTube have made the process of uploading videos easy and intuitive. If you want to upload a video, simply find the file on your device, fill in the description, keywords, and topics, then click upload. It's literally as simple as 1, 2, 3! The time it takes for the video to get completely uploaded would depend upon the size of the video's file and how fast your internet connection is. Once your video is completely uploaded, you will receive a notification via email. All the aspects of using YouTube are extremely easy. This is another reason why this site has exploded in popularity in such a short amount of time.

YouTube Risks and Safety Tips

Sure, YouTube is an amazing site where people can share, watch, like, upload, and comment on videos. It's a versatile video service which you can access through different devices such as smartphones, tablets, laptops, and desktop computers. Although people of all ages use YouTube, it's most popular among teenagers. This is because it's the perfect place for them to find things they like or they're really interested in. They can learn life hacks, watch shows, see the latest music videos, and so much more.

If you want to create an account on YouTube, you must be 18 years old and above. Users who are 13-17 years old need parental consent before they can create their own account. However, there may be some variations in the age restrictions depending on the country. As previously mentioned, you don't have to create an account to be able to gain access to the videos on the site. There is also a kid-friendly version of YouTube which is designed for younger audiences. This version makes it easy for parents to find content that their little ones are interested in.

Although YouTube is an excellent place to learn new things and find entertainment, it does come with some risks just like any other social media or sharing platform. The two main risks to watch out for are:

- **Unsuitable content**

  Since virtually anyone in the world can upload content on YouTube freely, some people may publish content which is unsuitable for children and teenagers. For parents, they can minimize this risk by flagging the content. If they see a video which they deem unsuitable or inappropriate, they can flag the video so it doesn't turn up again.

- **Cyberbullying**

  Sadly, cyberbullying can also happen on

YouTube. This mainly happens in the comments section of the videos. So if a child or a teenager has his own YouTube profile or YouTube channel, parents should monitor it constantly. Otherwise, their child might experience cyberbullying without their parents even knowing about it. The best thing to do is to disable the comment function on the channel or profile. It's easy to do this by changing the settings and it will greatly reduce the risk of the child receiving any negative comments. Also, if a parent discovers that his/her child is experiencing cyberbullying, there's an option to report and block users.

Although there are risks, there are also ways you can keep yourself and your children safe on YouTube. In this digital age, social media sites such as this one have already become a part of our lives. So rather than preventing your child from using YouTube, you may employ these helpful safety tips:

- **Manage the privacy settings**

  Whenever you would upload a video on YouTube, the default setting is public. This means that anyone with access to the internet can see the video. Depending on the child's age, manage the privacy settings to limit the number of people who can see what's being shared. It's easy to change the settings to unlisted or private if you want to prevent other people from seeing your child's uploaded content.

- **Setup the parental controls**

  Before allowing your child to use YouTube, make sure that you've setup the parental controls and age restrictions on the site. In doing this, you would have better control over your child's YouTube activity.

- **Disable the comment function**

  We've discussed how you can completely disable the comment function on YouTube videos. There's also an option to approve the comments first before they get published to the comments section. These are basic steps you can employ to prevent any form of cyberbullying on YouTube.

- **Utilize the safety mode**

  Finally, you can use the site's safety mode. This is a setting wherein you can prevent any mature content from showing up. It's one of the "opt-in" settings which means that you need to activate it so it will start working. The safety mode setting will filter any search results and exclude any videos which are age-restricted or mature content. Although there is no filtering system that's completely accurate. It's recommended to turn this setting on if you're planning to allow your child to use the site.

Some Interesting Facts About YouTube

Viewers all over the globe love accessing YouTube which is why it has become immensely popular. There's no way of telling what will go viral on YouTube as it would depend on what the users upload and which videos get shared over and over again. When it comes to this site, there's a lot to share, a lot to learn, and a lot to do. To add to your knowledge bank, here are some interesting facts about YouTube that you probably didn't know about:

- **The idea of YouTube came from former employees of Paypal**

  Back in 2005, three former employees of Paypal named Jawed Karim, Steve Chen, and Chad Hurley started YouTube. These three founders of the social media giant were working at Paypal when it was still an internet start-up. As a matter of fact, Chad Hurley created the logo when he learned about the company and emailed them to get hires. In the beginning, YouTube acquired its very first funds from the bonuses they received after the buyout of Paypal by eBay. One thing's for sure, if the executives of Paypal had any clue on what these former employees of theirs were about to create, they probably wouldn't have allowed them to go.

- **When YouTube started, it was actually meant as a dating site**

The first concept of YouTube was far from what it is today. In fact, there were some stories that it began as a dating site called "Tune In Hook Up." However, fate happened to have other plans for it as the founders decided to change that first concept. There were two important events which actually led to YouTube's creation.

First was when Jawed Kim, although looked everywhere, couldn't find any video footage of the wardrobe malfunction of Janet Jackson. Second was when Chad Hurley and Steve Chen couldn't share a dinner party footage due to the restrictions on email attachments. Because of these issues, they decided to go another way and thus, created the YouTube we know and love until today.

- **There was a time when YouTube was very problematic**

It's interesting to note that when YouTube first came out, it caused huge traffic for a company specializing in tube and roll form equipment. And this happened just because people who were curious about YouTube spelled the name wrong. Back in 2005, when they registered YouTube.com, people thought it was "utube.com" which, incidentally, belonged to a Universal Tube &Rollform Equipment Company in

Perrysburg, Ohio. Because of the error, the company experienced unexpected traffic which caused problems for them. The company even sued YouTube as they made allegations that their business sustained damages because of the video sharing site. Later on, the claims got dismissed and the company decided to use another domain name.

- **A zoo visit was the very first video which was uploaded on YouTube**

Now that we're all addicted to YouTube, it's kind of hard to remember which video was the very first that got uploaded to the site. Well, the very first video actually came from one of the founders, Jawed Karim. He shared video footage of his visit to a zoo in San Diego. The video featured Jawed standing in front of an elephant and it gained more than 4.2 million views when he published it on April 23, 2005.

- **YouTube's first Rickroll and its yearly April Fool's pranks**

A lot of people don't know this but every year, YouTube pranks it users each time April Fool's Day comes along. The very first prank happened on the site's homepage, which was a Rickroll. Back in the year 2009, YouTube inverted its entire website much to the surprise of its users. Since then, they began an April Fool's Day tradition wherein they think of new and surprising ways.

In the year 2008, the Rickroll was at its most popular and it was already considered a phenomenon. Today, this prank is still one of the most common online jokes used by websites. It's a kind of bait and switch which makes use of a hyperlink that has been disguised.

Chapter 2: Why Do People Love YouTube?

Since YouTube was launched, this media outlet has continuously been growing. Still, a lot of people wonder why it's so appealing. No matter how productive we want to be, once we start watching videos on YouTube, time flies by so fast and we're left with nothing but good memories of the things we've seen. Still, we end up feeling good about how we spent our time as one of the billions of YouTube viewers.

One of the main reasons why people go on YouTube is that it offers a wide variety of content. It's an amazing video platform for anyone around the world provided by users all over. This makes it easier for video creators to share their individualized content with a huge audience. Popular as it is, YouTube works around a very simple concept making it highly attractive to different kinds of people. Once you go on this site, you'll find out that there's a wide array of viewing options to choose from so you're sure to find something that will catch your interest and keep you hooked.

Another reason YouTube is very popular is that it provides a leisurely viewing experience. This is an essential factor in terms of entertainment. As long as you have access to the internet, you can watch the content on YouTube anytime and anywhere. The site is the perfect embodiment of leisurely watchability. And since you can also watch the videos from any device, you have all the content YouTube has to offer right at your fingertips.

YouTube has an extremely effective technique to keep its viewers coming back for more. Because it acknowledges the fact that there are audiences on the other side of the screen, this makes the site more personable. YouTube has a video layout that makes it more like a blog, hence giving it more of an edge over other mainstream media options. While you watch videos on YouTube, you can connect with the person who has created them on a more profound and more personal level. The content uploaded by users, especially the celebrities allow the viewers to take a peek into their minds.

Also, one of the best things about YouTube is that it's constantly offering new content. There are billions of YouTube channels available and users are always uploading new videos no matter where they are in the world. Because of this, people are always compelled to check out the site and find the most exciting and trending thing out there.

Understanding the Purpose of YouTube

The popular video sharing platform is all about getting viewers to keep on watching videos one after the other so that they can also see the ads embedded in those videos. But if you want to become a famous YouTuber, you shouldn't just think of the site as a collection of videos that's just waiting for your content to get added.

Instead, you should see YouTube as a type of social media platform where instead of having a profile, each user has his own channel. Whenever you add a video to your account, this becomes part of your channel. If your channel only contains a random collection of ads for your business, product or services, you probably won't get a lot of audiences. That is unless you're selling a really cool, cutting edge product such as a high-tech robot or something similar.

You can get the most out of YouTube if you have a really cool video which has the potential of going viral. This would happen if it's about something extremely amazing, something really funny or if you've created a series of short videos which will entertain or teach your target audiences. If your main goal is to explode on YouTube and become one of the most famous YouTubers ever, then you have to build a huge network of viewers and subscribers.

At its core, the main purpose of YouTube is to share videos. But since it became so popular, people have started earning money off the site which has become another great purpose. Before you can become a YouTube sensation, think about how you use the site first. When you're going through different video choices, one of the last things you'd probably click on is commercials. Realistically speaking, no matter how much you love something, you wouldn't want to spend a lot of time watching commercials about it. Instead, you would try to find something that's trending or something that you find really interesting. So no matter how much effort you place into making your commercials, people might not click on them.

YouTube is a free online video sharing site which has billions of users worldwide. Since Google owns this social media giant, you can be sure that it's well-indexed by its search engine. It also happens to be the most-used and most popular search engine in the entire world. So if you want to become famous on YouTube this 2019, you should think about all this information.

Even if your purpose is to grow your brand or business, you can also do this through YouTube. Possibly the best thing you can do is to pay for advertising on YouTube. On the site, you're likely to find your target market because almost everyone is on it anyway. So paying to advertise your business on the site makes a lot of sense. But if you're targeting a very specific type of audience, then YouTube might not be your best option. Even if you pay for advertising, you might just be showing your product or service off to people who aren't really interested in what you're selling. But for the purpose of building your brand on a larger scale, advertising on YouTube may help out a lot. This is especially true if you want to reach a lot of people and you have a very compelling ad to share with them.

The Reasons Why People Use YouTube

No matter where you live in the world, you would have probably heard about YouTube already. Although television has a lot to offer, YouTube offers unique content which you won't see anywhere else.

The first time YouTube was launched, people started using it immediately. Then just by word of mouth, they shared the news of the amazing new site and it spread like wildfire. The fact is, very little was spent or done to market YouTube and yet, it's now one of the biggest things on the internet. This just shows that the product didn't need advertising. It spoke for itself and it became a worldwide sensation all on its own.

No matter what type of video you'd like to view or share, you have the chance to do so on YouTube. Right now, there are a plethora of videos available on the site from those which entertain, teach, amuse, and so much more. If you're a business owner and you want to promote your brand, YouTube is an excellent tool to spread the word about what you have to offer without having to spend so much. It's also a great place to learn about new services or products available you can get your hands on.

If you create music and you want to showcase your talent, becoming famous on YouTube is the best way to go. You can film yourself playing music, upload your videos on YouTube for free and wait for them to go viral. Of course, after you've shared your video with the world, you may have to wait for some time and see how the public receives it.

For some people, the only reason they go on YouTube is to watch all of the videos either for educational or entertainment purposes. But if you want to get the most out of YouTube, you may want to create your own account.

Downloading and uploading videos is also easy on YouTube. Depending on your internet connection, both processes are relatively fast too. For some devices, you may have to install specific programs so that you can view the video content. Apart from this, all the other parts of the site are pretty much self-explanatory. It's easy to use YouTube which is why a lot of people love using it.

Why Do Videos on YouTube Go Viral?

We've already established that YouTube can be seen all over the world. Because of this, aspiring movie stars, musicians, and celebrity wannabes see the site as their chance to become famous and gain a lot of money. Of course, this perception didn't just appear without reason. A lot of people have already been discovered thanks to YouTube. This site is a means for you to reach a global audience which is much different from getting on local television. It also provides a simple way for you to use social media technology and social media marketing from anywhere in the world.

It's both a portal and a platform which nobody in social media history ever expected to come about. It has a unique scale, reach, and size which sets it apart from any other video sharing site. It provides users with face to face communication along with its emotional nuance and power. Billions of people all over the world use the site each and every day. Also, it provides more than 4 billion hours of videos for users to enjoy and for every minute that passes by, more than 70 hours of videos get uploaded. This site is the perfect place to upload content if you want an audience to gain access to it. For those who want to become famous, the challenge is to come up with content that will go viral.

Brent Coker, a professor of marketing claims that he has discovered an algorithm which may explain why some videos go viral and others don't. It may also explain why people will watch some videos and won't even bother clicking on others. He named this algorithm of his the "Branded Viral Movie Predictor" and it includes four essential elements which are emotive strength, congruency, network involvement, and paired meme strategy. As proof of this, one of the examples he had cited to prove this algorithm was the YouTube video of QuikSilver which went viral back in 2007.

Supposedly, this formula can break down the science behind sharing into a single equation.

However, scientists don't really have this concept within their grasp yet. Despite this, it still provides some valuable insight and as research continues, who knows what they will discover in the future? What we do know for sure is that there are a few reasons why some videos go viral.

A video may go viral instantly when Tastemakers share it. These are social media influencers who have a huge following. They introduce the public to new, interesting things which help grow their audience even more. One of the earliest examples of this phenomenon happened back in 2010. The talkshow host Jimmy Kimmel who had more than 1.6 million followers on Twitter tweeted about one of the "funniest videos in the world." A few months before that, a user known as Yosemite Mountain Bear uploaded that particular video on YouTube and nobody really noticed it. But when Jimmy Kimmel's tweet came out and a huge audience saw it, the video exploded all over the internet and gained more than 35 million views. With this example alone, you can see how much of a difference Tastemakers can make!

Another thing which helps make videos go viral is communities of participation. One of the best examples which shows this concept is the music video entitled "Friday" by Rebecca Black. When the would-be musician uploaded the video, it only gained a couple of views and didn't generate much of a reaction. However, a couple of blogs became interested in the video. Because of this, a wide range of online communities began recreating their own version of Rebecca Black's video. Now, the video has more than 10,000 parodies on YouTube!

These days, people create parodies of trending videos each and every day. Then the original video along with all of the remixed versions will start going viral. Pretty soon, Tastemakers will see these videos and share them to their audiences which, in turn, will speed up the process significantly. At the end of the day, it would be as if the online communities who have viewed, shared, and created videos will all be sharing one huge inside joke. For the past years now, people don't just view videos passively. Instead, we are able to actively participate in the process by creating new videos.

Finally, another big reason why videos go viral is unexpectedness. There are times when people feel passionately about something they want to protest, and they share that online. Then the people who feel the same way as the one who shared the original video will talk about it and keep on sharing it. The process goes on and on until we all see it explode on YouTube and gain millions of views. Simple as this principle may seem, it applies to a lot of the videos which have gone viral.

How Can People Make Money on YouTube?

By far, the easiest and most common way people can earn money on YouTube is via paid product placement and advertising. For some people, they earn on YouTube by allowing ads to play before their video plays. These users open an AdSense account on Google and it keeps track of the number of impressions the video gets. Impressions refer to the number of times a video gets watched for more than 30 seconds. Earning on AdSense is based on how many impressions a video has, which ads are played before the video, and how many times users click on the ads. As soon as the account earns $100, the payment gets sent to the user.

Others choose to utilize paid product placement which is another method for monetizing a YouTube account. This method of earning happens when a YouTube user gets a sponsor to pay him to review a feature or product within his video. Generally, the more viewers watch a particular video, the more valuable it is to the sponsor or the advertiser. In such a case, the user has a higher chance of earning more revenue through paid product placement. If you want to choose this method, you need to make sure that you have a huge audience who will keep on watching your videos all the way to the end.

The best way a user can appeal to a large group of audiences is by employing some strategic YouTube practices. Keep in mind that most viewers are interested in getting entertained or educated on the site through the videos. So if you want to attract a lot of subscribers and earn money on YouTube, make sure you're creating rich and engaging content all the time. This will ensure that your videos will always get viewed and shared by your target audiences. The more engaging a video is, the more valuable it is to the site and to those who are interested in advertising.

However, no matter how engaging your content is, there's still a chance that you may run into challenges in terms of generating revenue. For one, the average rate paid for pre-roll ads is significantly lower than the rate paid for more traditional media outlets. Also, you would have to deal with the costs of producing a high-quality video along with the advertising profits that YouTube collects. Still, a lot of people choose to make a career on YouTube and get successful.

Chapter 3: Creating Your Own YouTube Channel

Now that you've learned more about YouTube, the next step is to learn how to create your own channel on the site. If you want to become a famous YouTuber in 2019, you can't do it without opening your own account and starting your channel. When you employ the right strategies, you can explode in popularity, taking your brand right along with you.

If you've been itching to share your brand or yourself to the world but you don't know where to start, don't worry. It may seem overwhelming at first but we have already established how YouTube is extremely simple and easy to use. Before you begin, you should think about what name to use for your channel. This is the very first step because once you've registered that name, changing it is more trouble than it's worth. So decide whether you want to use your personal name for your channel or the name of your business, if you have one. Think about something unique, something which will make a huge first impression and something which you will stick with from here on out.

After that, you need to setup your Gmail and Google Plus accounts. Although these are outside of YouTube, setting up these accounts is part of the process so it's best to get them over with. The good news is that these two things occur seamlessly together. So if you want your channel to have its own Gmail and Google Plus accounts, set them up that way. Or if you already have these accounts, you can also use them for your channel.

Next up, it's time to create your cover art and decide which profile picture to use. You need to upload your profile picture into your Google Plus account too. This is actually why you need this account in the first place. Then upload your cover art the same way and it will appear on YouTube as well. After getting these things out of the way, it's time for the fun part: creating your content and uploading it on YouTube for everyone to see!

YouTube Channel Basics

Although there are hundreds of thousands of blogs and sharing sites all over the internet, none of them come close to the popularity YouTube has gained since it first came about. If you want the world to know you, your business or your brand, then YouTube is the hottest place to be in right now. Let's go through the basics of launching your own YouTube channel.

Planning

Just like any other endeavor, one of the first things you need to do is make some plans. Think about what your channel will be all about. Of course, you would like to create content that people will want to see. Videos which they will watch over and over again and will make the audiences wanting more. But the videos you produce should also come naturally to you. They should be relevant to yourself or your business.

Right now, some of the most common types of videos people on YouTube are sharing include:

- How-to / instructional videos

- Interviews with the experts in different industries

- Comedic videos

- Reviews of products or services

- Information on how you can use a specific product

- Re-publishing podcasts

There are so many other types of videos you can create. If you can think of a unique type of video which you think people haven't seen before, that would be even better! Part of the planning stage would be setting up your account which we have already discussed in the previous section. After you've finished this step, it's time to start optimizing your channel.

Optimization

When you optimize your YouTube channel, it will help increase your likelihood of success in terms of social media marketing. Add your logo or your profile photo, your cover image, and the description of your channel. You can easily do this by clicking on the "My Channel" button. When you're adding these elements to your channel's profile, make sure that everything stands out. Also, make sure that the description you place accurately talks about the content you plan to publish. Otherwise, this might mislead the viewers which, in turn, might end up disappointing them. If you have your own website, you can even add the link to your channel's description.

Uploading videos

After setting everything up, it's time to start uploading your videos. These will be the content of your channel. By this time, you should already have a couple of videos on your device to upload.

To publish content, just select the video from your device and upload it on YouTube. You also have to create an interesting description for each of your videos so the viewers can find out what they're all about before viewing.

Setting up your playlists

After you've uploaded a couple of videos, you can now setup your playlist. A playlist is simply a collection of videos which play one after the other in a specific arrangement. If you want your viewers to watch your videos in a specific order, then this is an important step.

Simple as it is, creating your own YouTube channel is a great opportunity for you to reach your target audience. As you can see, setting up the channel is very easy and it would only take a couple of minutes. From there, you can learn more about YouTube as you go along.

What is a YouTube Channel?

Anyone who registers on YouTube can make their own channel on the site. This will serve as the homepage for your account. After you've setup your account, your channel will show you the basic information including your account name, your personal description, public videos, member uploads, and any other information which you've entered. Also, you have the option to customize the color scheme and background of your personal channel. You can also manage the information which appears to the public. Businesses can also have their own channels which are different from the personal channels created by individuals. If you want to make your brand famous, then you should sign up for a Brand Account.

YouTube Personal Channel

Although anyone can watch videos on YouTube even without having their own account, you can only create your personal channel by signing up.

This is also an important step if you want to use all the features of the site such as uploading videos, adding comments or creating your own video playlists. You can use the same login information on your personal YouTube account as on the rest of your Google accounts. So if you already have existing Google accounts such as Gmail, Google Drive, Google Plus, and others, signing up would be a lot easier.

YouTube Business Channel

If you want to create a YouTube channel for your business, then you should open a Brand Account. For this type of account, it would be better to create a separate Google account or you can use the same login information as your business' Google account if it already has one. If different people will be able to access this account, you have to provide them with the login details too.

Just like other social media sites, your YouTube channel serves as your personal presence on the site. So if someone wants to learn more about you, he can click on your name and go through your channel. Conversely, you can also learn more about people and businesses by visiting their channels, reading their descriptions, and watching the videos which they have already uploaded.

Tips for Creating Your Own YouTube Channel

The Google-owned video site boasts billions of users all over the globe and that doesn't even include those who use the site but didn't sign up. If you're planning to start your own channel and make it grow, let's take a look at some helpful tips for creating your own YouTube channel:

- Make sure to identify the target audience you plan to reach through your channel. This is an important part of the planning stage. Apart from deciding what your channel is all about, you also have to know what type of viewers you would like your channel to cater to. That way, you will have a better idea of how you will plan your content.

- Differentiate yourself from the competition by finding a niche where you know you're really good at. You should be able to provide high-quality, interesting content if you've selected a niche which you have a lot of knowledge on.

- Create a schedule for producing your content. Just because you've already uploaded a few videos on your channel, that doesn't mean your work stops there, especially if you plan to be the next YouTube sensation in 2019. You have to keep on coming up with new videos according to the trends you see and what your viewers are asking for. This will keep your audiences loyal to your channel.

- Optimization doesn't stop with your channel. You also have to do this for your channel's content so when people perform searches, your channel will always come up. When it comes to this type of optimization, just think of the same considerations as traditional search optimization. This means that you have to include some target keywords in the descriptions and the titles of each of your videos. Also, pay attention to your video's comments, likes, and how it is categorized. As you gain more audiences and subscribers, you will learn more about what works and what doesn't.

- Adding links to your channel can be very effective too, especially if you have a personal or business website which you'd like to promote in your videos.

- Channel trailers can be really cool too so when visitors come to your channel, they can have a preview of the content you're offering and why they should subscribe. A short channel trailer can introduce the viewers to your content and encourage them to check out the rest of your content.

- Include your contact details on your channel too, especially if it's a business channel. Do this so your viewers can get in touch with you directly in case they want to learn more.

Apart from the basic steps we've discussed in the previous section, these pointers can help you create a more effective YouTube channel to start you off. The more active you are on YouTube, the faster you'll learn about the ins and outs of the business. As time goes by, you will learn what your target audience is looking for and what they're not really interested in based on how many views your videos get and other relevant factors.

Ensuring the Success of Your YouTube Channel

After you've employed all of the tips and steps for

setting up your YouTube channel, your work doesn't stop there. You have to keep people engaged if you want them to keep coming back for more. To ensure the success of your YouTube channel, you have to constantly maintain it and keep it updated.

Finding your angle

Monitor all of the videos that you post on your channel. See which ones go viral and which ones are ignored. Do this so you can find the best angle to maintain the loyalty of your viewers. Also, keep these things in mind:

- Authentic content works better than "glossy" corporate videos. Even if you're managing a business channel, trends show that people are more attracted to genuine videos compared to the ones which seem scripted or forced.

- Think about what you want, what's trending, and the type of videos which go viral. You don't have to copy these exactly but you can get a lot of valuable insights from such videos.

- All of your videos should inspire people to have positive feelings no matter what they're about. If you just talk about yourself or your business, you might end up boring your audience.

- Usually, short videos which come out frequently are more interesting than long-winded ones which only come out every month or so.

- Think about all the aspects of your content. For instance, you're promoting a business which sells electronics. That doesn't mean that all of your videos should be about electronic products. Think about other interesting concepts such as troubleshooting, the newest electronic gadgets to look out for, and more.

- The same thing goes for when you have

your personal channel. Let's say the main content you have on your channel is about makeup tutorials. Once in a while, why not insert some product reviews? Or some makeup removal hacks that work? Inserting such content will make your audiences interested in seeing what you have in store for them next.

Planning your content

Planning your content is a constant process. Since you will be monitoring your videos and how your audiences accept them, you may have to make some changes in your initial plans. You might find out that viewers aren't really interested in a specific type of video you've published and you've seen this trend a few times. In such case, you should think of new content to inspire and engage your audiences. If you see some videos that your viewers watch over and over again, think about new content which you will present in the same way.

Producing your videos

Most people who plan to create their own channel on YouTube to upload videos already have a lot of experience in filming. But if this is your first time, you might feel a bit overwhelmed. Again, this is a learning process. You don't have to be a professional to upload videos on YouTube. In fact, your viewers might even appreciate you more when they see how you grow and improve as time goes by. When producing your videos, consider these pointers:

- In the beginning, utilize whatever equipment you already have or anything that you can afford. Using basic equipment is better than nothing and as time goes by and you're earning from the videos you're producing, you can purchase more equipment to produce content of a higher quality.

- It's best to use natural lighting when shooting videos. This means going outdoors when it's sunny. Ordinary indoor lighting seldom looks good when uploaded on YouTube.

- A lapel microphone is a must-have, affordable item which you need from the beginning. You can purchase a cheap one first then buy a better one after you've gained from your channel.

- Don't take things too seriously. If you have any funny slip-ups, you can even compile these in a single video and upload that for the entertainment of your viewers. That way, they will see you as a real person instead of someone who never makes mistakes.

Uploading, promoting, and getting involved

Uploading your video to the site is a very simple process. But if you want your video to turn up when people perform searches, you may have to do some keyword research. YouTube offers its own keyword tool which may help you out. Knowing the right keywords to use will help make your content more popular, reaching especially those who are actually looking for what you want to provide.

Promoting is a huge part of YouTube, especially for those who want to become famous. Ideally, your video should get a good number of views early on after it gets uploaded. To do this, you can embed your video on your other social media sites or your personal blog. In the beginning, you may have to do a lot of self-promotion. But the more famous you get, the more people will talk about you and do the promoting for you.

Finally, you should always involve yourself with your channel, your audiences, and your subscribers. Sharing, commenting, and responding to comments will keep your videos active which, in turn, may help grow your profile. The more active your channel is, the more people will learn about it and become interested in it. This doesn't just apply to your own channel.

Involve yourself with other channels as well. Subscribe to channels which interest you, comment on trending videos, and more. Doing all of this will help you become even more known in the YouTube world.

Chapter 4: Getting Educated on YouTube

A few years ago, YouTube may have just started out as a place to share videos for the purpose of entertainment. But now, more and more people are going on the site to get educated. Although there are still hundreds of thousands of entertaining videos available, most of us are now interested to learn new skills and new information on the video sharing site.

In this modern world, we would often find ourselves in situations wherein we would have to accomplish a task but we have no idea where to start or how to do it. Fortunately, you can go on YouTube for some self-directed learning. A lot of viewers use this site to help them out in such situations. If you need to learn more for school, for work, or for your hobbies, there's a very high chance of finding what you're looking for on YouTube.

And we're not talking about simply brushing up on the skills that you already possess. Although a lot of people do this, many also turn to YouTube to learn a skill that they don't have. So if you want to spend your free time productively, you can go on the site and search for a couple of interesting videos which will help enhance your skills!

It's Fun to Learn on YouTube

YouTube's video collection can help any curious person learn new things in interesting ways. For instance, you may find videos on how to make your own birdhouse to hang in one of the trees in your backyard. Or you may want to learn how to make parodies of the most famous music videos. You can even go on YouTube to watch thousands of videos about life hacks! From amateur videos to professional ones, you won't run out of choices from YouTube's treasure trove.

As soon as people realized that they can upload educational videos on the site, they did just that.

In fact, there was a surplus of these types of videos on the site back in 2009. The creators came up with YouTube EDU which was a specific location where users could upload all of their educational content. Now with more than 700,000 videos and counting, people all over the world can learn just about anything. Also, teachers and schools are now making YouTube part of the learning process of their students.

Just because YouTube is an excellent source of educational videos, that doesn't mean that teachers should get "video-happy" and only use the site for teaching their students. Combining the traditional learning techniques with a few YouTube "bonuses" would be a great way to keep their students interested in what they're learning. There are a lot of universities now which create their own account to post lectures and share them online. Doing this allows the professors and instructors to share their educational content, collaborate with other educators, and learn more creative ways to teach their lessons. No matter how you look at it, YouTube helps make learning fun for everyone!

How to Make a Superb Educational Channel on YouTube

On the other side of the coin, instead of wanting to learn from YouTube, you might want to share what you know about it. To do this, you need to create educational content and share it on your own educational channel. For a comprehensive guide on how to do this, you may refer to the EDU Playbook Guide which was released by YouTube. But since learning this concept can also help you become famous on YouTube this 2019, let's have a quick look at how you can create a superb channel for the purpose of educating your viewers.

Select an education channel category

The site categorizes its education channels into four main groups namely:

- Pre-K (these include channels such as Yo

Gabba Gabba and Sesame Street)

- Primary and Secondary (these include channels such as Khan Academy)

- Higher Education (these include channels like MIT)

- Lifelong Learning (these include channels like Big Think)

Think about the category you want your channel to be placed in and select that.

Select the style of your educational content

There are two main styles of educational content you can create namely:

- Academic which is more straightforward and formal.

- Edutainment which is entertainment-based and has a more casual feel.

Choosing the style of your educational content is

important so you can reach your target audience. For instance, if you want to reach an academic group of people but you produce videos with an edutainment style, your viewers might not take you too seriously. Conversely, if you want to reach a wider range of people, those who want to learn random skills and information, sharing videos with an academic style might bore them or put them off which, in turn, would lead them to look for other more engaging content.

Think about the scope of your educational content

You can create the scope of your content in two main ways namely:

- Full lesson videos where you will plan the whole series of your videos from start to finish. So each video you upload would be part of the whole topic and as time goes by, you will be providing your audiences with educational content for them to learn a whole course. When making this type of content, you may want to create a playlist for all your videos so any new viewers can play them in the right order.

- Supplemental videos, on the other hand, don't offer a lot of details. Instead, they would provide the viewers with additional information about a topic, a concept or a subject.

Consider your strategy for EDU Programming

Again, you have different options to choose from when strategizing for your EDU Programming.

- Lesson or Course videos are a series of videos which you would create to give your viewers a more profound coverage of what you're teaching. So you would have to think about how you will break down the whole subject and present each of the topics to your viewers.

  If you plan to use this type of strategy, you

need to organize all of your content well. Ideally, your viewers should be able to navigate your playlists and your channel easily. For instance, if a new viewer visits your channel because he wants to learn a whole course, he should be able to find the very first video of that course without much effort.

- By contrast, self-contained videos would only be about a single topic. For these types of videos, you can make different ones which focus on separate topics then share them with your viewers.

For this type of strategy, you have to make sure that the videos you share are topical and they focus on major events which are happening all over the world. This will make them more relevant to the viewers.

Choose your instruction strategy

There are so many different methods you can use to teach people. If you want to encourage your audience to keep on coming back for more, you should:

- Talk about the common misconceptions. Some of the most-viewed videos on YouTube are the ones which address misconceptions and provide concrete evidence of why these ideas just aren't true.

- Make use of different examples and approaches when you're teaching a single concept. This will make it easier for different types of people to understand the lesson you're trying to teach.

- Using visual aids would be an excellent way to support your viewers' learning. Also, visuals can help simplify the concept and make it more understandable to the people who are watching.

Tips for producing better content

If you want people to enjoy your videos while still

being able to learn from them, you have to come up with superior content. Remember that there are billions of videos on YouTube and chances are, there would be a lot of them which would also be teaching the same things you want to teach. Therefore, you have to make sure that your channel stands out. Here are some tips to do that:

- Try your best to hook your viewer early on. You can do this by giving a "teaser" of the lesson's final product or by presenting an intriguing question at the start of the video.

- Edit the video before you upload it. Watch the whole thing and try to gauge whether it's interesting enough or not. If needed, cut out some parts, insert a few supplemental clips, and more.

- Include a call to action somewhere in the video. This is any statement which will get your viewer more involved in your channel and not just in the video he's watching.

- Shoot the video from several camera angles. That way, the viewer will get different perspectives and won't feel like he's just listening to a person talking in front of him.

- In terms of long-form content, you might want to consider condensing your content into a shorter video which only focuses on the most relevant parts. If you create videos which are too long, your viewers might not watch them all the way to the end. That is unless you have a video that's really compelling and you're sure that it will hold the attention of your viewers from start to end.

Apply "Tent-Pole Programming" to your channel

"Tent-Pole Programming" refers to a type of strategy wherein you create educational content that's relevant or even trending at the time when you create it. When employing this strategy, keep these in mind:

- Do your research and think about educational content you can create for what's trending and for topical events. This will make your video relevant and exciting to those looking for more information on these topics.

- You can also create educational content that's related to the coming holidays. For instance, when Thanksgiving is approaching, you can make "how-to" videos on how to set the perfect Thanksgiving table.

- After creating a couple of videos about these topics, create a tent-pole playlist so your viewers can watch all of the videos one after the other.

Don't forget the interaction

Apart from sharing videos to your audience, you

would also want them to understand what you're teaching more fully, learn more of the same concept or learn other topics, and interact with you. The start of this journey happens with your video but it shouldn't end there. You want your channel to be more than just a passive viewing experience for your followers. To do this, you can:

- Create interactive videos. In such videos, you can ask a question then take your viewers to a different part of your video based on their response. Either that or you can take your viewers to an entirely different video. This will encourage your viewers to think while they're learning and not just watch the video passively.

- Encourage your viewers to continue learning outside of your YouTube channel. You can direct them to different sites and social media platforms where they can learn more about the topic you're teaching.

Tools Which Can Help You Create Amazing Educational Videos on YouTube

Apart from using your own skills to create amazing educational videos for your channel, there are some tools available which may help improve your content. For some tools, you would have to pay to use them while others are totally free-of-charge. To give you a better idea of what's out there, here are a few tools which can be a great help for educational videos:

Go!Animate

This tool will help you create your own cartoons easily. Simply personalize the characters, select the scenarios for your characters to move in, then record your narration or use text speech for your characters' conversations. This is a fun tool to use for teaching kids.

One True Media

This is one of the most robust video editors available online. It comes with plenty of transition effects, it's easy to edit photos and video clips, and you can also insert music and text overlays. This tool has an interface that's user-friendly but it allows you to create professional-looking videos.

Stupeflix

This is a type of digital scrapbook. You would choose one of the formats then just add your videos or photos by dragging and dropping them. Other features include adding text, a speech feature for narration, maps, and music. This is an excellent tool for when you're teaching history, geography or similar subjects.

Teaching Audiences Online

You can find a wealth of content which can help you learn more and make you a more-skilled individual. Among all of the videos available on the site, you can find some great content which will teach you some new skills such as:

Building computers

Rather than purchasing a computer set and spending a lot of money on it, you can actually build one with the help of YouTube. This skill will help you spend less while learning a valuable skill which might even be helpful for you in the long-run. By learning how to build computers according to your preferred specs, you will also learn more about these machines and how to troubleshoot them in case you run into any problems.

Cooking

For whatever reason, you may want to improve your culinary skills. This is an easy topic to find on YouTube. From finding recipes online to videos which actually show how to prepare and cook the dish, there's a lot to learn in terms of cooking. You can even search for a specific dish and find a lot of videos on how to cook that dish in different ways.

Foreign languages

It's a lot easier to learn how to speak foreign languages now thanks to YouTube. Again, you will find a lot of videos online which will help you learn the basics. This skill will come in handy if you're planning to travel to a foreign land and you want to be able to communicate with the locals.

Home repairs

DIY videos are extremely popular on YouTube these days. Whether you just want to save some money on repairs or you really want to learn how to fix things up at home, you can find different videos on the site which can help you out. Of course, there are still some repairs which require a professional touch so try to gauge whether you can do the job yourself or not. Otherwise, you might end up spending more than what you would have spent if you hired a professional from the beginning.

Painting and drawing

Although YouTube won't magically give you innate talent, you can learn a lot about painting and drawing through videos. The great thing about this is that you can learn only what you want to learn. For instance, if you only want to learn how to doodle, then search for videos which teach that.

Photography

Anybody can learn this skill with ease through YouTube. You can search for videos which teach photography techniques based on the camera or gadget that you own. That way, you can learn more about what you have and start clicking photos like a professional!

Playing instruments

No matter what type of instrument you want to learn, you will find self-help videos on YouTube. You can also learn how to play the instruments using different styles. Keep on learning and you can become a pro in no time!

Self-defense

This is another helpful skill which you can learn on YouTube during your free time. These days, we should all learn how to defend ourselves so we're ready when the need arises. There are a lot of self-defense videos you can learn from depending on your own skills and physical capabilities.

Chapter 5: Getting Entertained on YouTube

The actual process of creating your own channel on YouTube only take a couple of minutes, but when it comes to customizing your channel to entertain your audiences, that takes more time and effort. While half of the users are learning on YouTube, the other half use the site for entertainment purposes. It's easy to get lost in the world of YouTube while watching video after video of funny animals, celebrity scandals, fun facts, and so much more.

The Art of Entertaining Audiences Through YouTube

It seems like YouTube has become something of a phenomenon in such a short period of time. When it first came out in 2005 and one of the founders uploaded his first video, nobody could have ever imagined how big it would become a few years later. But Google saw its potential only a year and a half after that first video came out. At that time, Google made an announcement that it was going to pay $1.65 billion to own the site.

Since that event, the influence and the power of YouTube have grown at an amazing speed. It even holds the title of the second biggest searching site in the world right after Google. What calls audiences to YouTube is the chance to be entertained by different videos shared by those who own the channels. People love watching these videos and for those who are producing the content, they are learning the art of entertaining different types of audiences through the video-sharing site.

Factors to Consider Before Creating an Entertainment Channel on YouTube

It's never too late to start your own YouTube channel. Each day, someone somewhere in the world is doing just that. The social media platform is currently booming despite there being some controversies about it. But before you create a channel on the site for the purpose of entertainment, you need to consider a few factors to ensure its success. If you want fame to be in your horizon this 2019, think about these factors:

What motivates you

Think about why you want to start an entertainment channel on YouTube. Your motivation will be your main driving force. Without it, you might lose interest somewhere along the way and end up neglecting your channel after some time has passed. Also, your motivation will be the basis for the most important elements of your YouTube channel which are:

- What your video content will be about

- Who you want your videos to attract

- Why your target audience should tune in to your videos

Establish your motivation as well as these three elements before you launch your entertainment channel. If not, you might end up with a channel full of random videos with no chance of capturing meaningful viewership. And without this, you won't ever see yourself becoming a famous YouTuber.

How often you will upload content on your channel

After deciding what type of content you will upload and who your target audience is, you also have to consider how often you will upload content. Usually, this would depend on the types of videos you will produce:

- For Let's Plays and vlogs, you may have to upload one video each day.

- For trivia videos which require a lot of research, once a week would be ideal.

- For skits, once a month would be adequate.

To ensure your success, you have to think long-term and always be realistic. You may have a lot of energy and excitement now but will you be able to sustain that for the next few months or years? If you want to focus on becoming famous on YouTube, then you have to commit to uploading content regularly for your viewers.

Style and substance

These two factors are essential for anyone who wants to create a successful channel on YouTube. You need to think of smart titles, come up with consistent formats, and make amazing video thumbnails. If your videos will also involve audio, make sure to work on the confidence in your voice, articulation, and staying away from irritating speech patterns. If you plan to appear on camera yourself, you have to look confident, steady, and you need to speak naturally without fidgeting or having awkward pauses. After filming, you also need to edit your videos properly before uploading them on the site.

Equipment needed for producing videos

If you just want to create random videos and upload them, then you can work with the equipment that you already own. But if you want to be really successful, you need the proper equipment such as:

- A high-quality camera. This can be a webcam or the camera of your smartphone. As long as it produces high-resolution videos, it's good enough.

- A tripod, especially if you're using a smartphone for filming.

- An external microphone so you can record the audio separately. Then during editing, you can combine the video and the audio for a more professional result.

- A green screen is important if you want to be able to have different backgrounds or add special effects without leaving the comfort of your home.

- Some type of Screen Capture Software would be helpful too if the videos you plan to upload involve screen capturing.

Promotional strategies

Success on YouTube depends on how well you promote your content. If you want to become famous this 2019, you have to do the work. Here are some great promotional strategies to consider:

- Build a following on social media so they can also follow you on YouTube.

- Find online forums and communities which are relevant to your channel. Then share your best content once in a while to get the members interested.

- Collaborate with other YouTubers to expand your network and your audience database.

Just like maintaining your channel, promoting

yourself is a long-term process. In fact, you might even have to wait for a few months or even a few years before you achieve true fame on the site. If you want to reach your goal, you need to persevere and never, ever give up.

YouTube monetization

It was much easier to make money on YouTube in the past. But that doesn't mean that this is an impossible venture today. There's a common misconception that YouTubers can earn a lot of money through advertisements. But the hard reality is that ads don't pay as much as the effort you put into producing your videos. So even if your channel or your videos go viral, don't expect to become rich overnight. Those who successfully earn money on YouTube do so by employing different YouTube monetization methods such as:

- Affiliate product and sales promotions

- Consultation services

- Advertisements which aren't Adsense

- Public speaking

- Donations from fans who support the channel

Realistic goals

The fastest way to lose hope on YouTube is to compare your channel with others. Instead of doing this, set some realistic goals for yourself and focus on them. Although your main goal may be to become a famous YouTuber in 2019, create smaller, actionable goals which will help you attain the final one. Your goals have to be measurable, have an achievable deadline, and should be things which you can accomplish based on your own skills. After you've reached the small goals you have set for yourself, keep on creating new ones until you reach your final goal of achieving fame and fortune.

How to Make a Compelling Entertainment Channel on YouTube

Since YouTube came out, it became part of our lives and it looks like it's here to stay. Videos, even those meant to entertain, play a huge part in social media marketing which means that YouTube plays a huge role too. Apart from social media platforms, videos have become a sort of sub-trend which is why they often go viral. Because of this, YouTube has grown bigger than ever as more and more people create their own channels to share what they know, their interests, and their discoveries to entertain audiences all over the world.

Probably the most engaging kinds of YouTube videos are the ones which are heartwarming, funny or global. The video contents that usually go trending are those which have a more personal nature rather than the political or corporate videos. These popular videos have acquired millions of views all over the world and they come from some of the most popular entertainment channels. If you want to join the ranks of these YouTube stars, try following these effective strategies:

Employ a social, multi-channel approach

The most famous YouTubers don't just promote themselves on the site. In order to grow their audience and build a loyal community, they make themselves known on other social networks too. This is especially important if you plan to share your entertainment channel with a purpose of marketing your brand or your business too.

Prioritize your social networks based on your target audience

After signing up on different social media platforms, you should also stay active in all of them. Of course, this can be very challenging, especially if you have a day job too. So what you can do is try to determine which of these networks have the majority of your followers. Then prioritize those networks by spending more time on them. For instance, if you notice that apart from YouTube, you get a lot of likes and comments on your FB posts whenever you share your videos there, then you should make Facebook your priority. But don't forget the others! You should still visit your other social networks regularly even if it's not that often.

Upload videos consistently, especially on your top channels

Merely "showing up" on your social media networks isn't enough. You have to interact with your fans and followers and keep them engaged by sharing and posting consistently. Otherwise, your followers might lose interest in you. If you had a great start and people are loving the videos you create, use that momentum. Forgetting to upload or not having anything to upload for some time will leave your audiences hanging but not hooked. Then when some other channel on YouTube starts trending, your followers might move on to that one.

Create engaging video content and upload right away

Any YouTuber who wants to keep his audiences loyal to his entertainment channel should make sure that all the content he creates is engaging. If you want to entertain audiences, the key is keeping them engaged. There's no YouTube star out there who has ever created boring or mundane videos. By this time, you should already have a good idea of the type of content you want to create as well as your target audience. So you should always think of new ways and new ideas to entertain your viewers and attract more of them to subscribe to your channel. Right after you've filmed your videos and edited them, make sure to upload those videos right away. And make sure to share those videos with your other social networks for the benefit of your other fans.

Leverage your content while you adapt it to the different social channels

One of the more common mistakes committed by

wannabe YouTubers is not leveraging their content across the different social channels. This is an important step to take if you want to become famous across the globe. Leveraging your content means that you promote your videos on the different social channels while also creating unique video content that's relevant to each of them. You may use similar topics which build upon each other but make sure that the specific video content you create has to vary depending on what works on each of the channels.

Entertaining Audiences Online

The term "entertainment" has a broad meaning, especially when you look at it in terms of YouTube channels. There are different types of entertainment channels on YouTube and they cater to different types of audiences. After all, what may be entertaining for one person might not be too appealing for another. This is why some entertainment channels explode in popularity while others don't. The popularity of this type of channel would depend on the quality of its content and how big of an audience the channel has.

Just like the most famous comedians, a lot of famous YouTubers who have entertainment channels become popular thanks to their self-deprecating and humorous take on the problems we all face each and every day. The key to starting your own entertainment channel on YouTube is to discover your own distinct style. Any aspiring entertainer can become famous by coming up with an amazingly unique idea that will speak to an audience no matter where they are in the world.

If you're planning to start your own YouTube channel, you should know exactly what type of entertainment videos to create. There are endless possibilities to consider and all you have to do is make a firm decision on what type you would like to produce and share with the world. To give you a better idea, here are some types of entertainment videos you can choose from:

Animation

If you have mad animation skills, then you can create your own short movies and cartoons to upload on your channel. Entertain audiences with heartwarming shorts which you have animated by yourself. Of course, creating this type of content takes a lot of effort since you have to think about the characters, the storylines, and all other elements of a good story. But if you're able to create great content, such videos will surely start trending!

Cooking Channels

Videos which show how cakes or dishes are being made can be really entertaining, especially if you're interested in cooking. So if you have a passion for cooking and you know how to make very interesting and visually-appealing dishes, you can start a channel and upload this type of content.

DIY and How To Channels

Although you can also learn a lot from these types of channels, they can also be extremely entertaining. Think about it, how many times have you watched "lifehack" videos or those which show you how to solve mundane problems? These types of videos can be very entertaining, especially when you're also learning new things in the process.

Edutainment

We've already talked about educational channels in our previous chapter but some of them can also be categorized under the entertainment category. If you want to make learning fun, then you can create an entertainment channel which also teaches valuable lessons. These types of channels are very common for children since they learn better and faster when it's done in a fun, exciting way.

Gaming Channels

These types of YouTube channels are very popular on YouTube. There are so many types of games available and players all over the world tune in regularly to gaming channels to enhance their gaming experiences. You can make reaction videos, walkthroughs, game reviews, and more depending on how much you know about the most popular games played by different types of audiences.

Music Channels

If you're an aspiring musician with a passion for dancing, singing, songwriting, creating music, and playing instruments then starting a music channel would be perfect for you. You can showcase your talents for all the world to see. Some of the most famous YouTubers create music channels and gain a lot of global fans thanks to their viewers, likers, and subscribers.

Stand Up Comedy

Funny people are the most entertaining types of people out there. This is why a lot of famous YouTubers are comedians. If you think you can entertain audiences with your humor, then you can try starting your own stand up comedy channel.

Vlogs

These types of videos are perfect for people who want to share their experiences and tell their stories to the world. Vlogs are video blogs which can be nostalgic, fun, poignant, or comedic in nature. When creating vlogs, you might chronicle your everyday life, capture some of your most special moments or even tell the world about your new experiences. By producing these types of videos, you can provide new and unique perspectives on the most mundane events.

These are some of the most common types of entertainment channels you can start on YouTube. There are a lot more! You can even think of a unique type of entertainment to share with audiences, one they haven't seen yet.

Chapter 6: How to Grow and Scale Your YouTube Channel

Think about this: When was the last time you watched a video on YouTube? Most people watch videos each and every day. This is why it's the perfect time to start a channel if you don't have your own yet. Even if you already have an existing channel but you haven't grown or scaled it yet, this is also the time to take some action. If you want to become a famous YouTuber in 2019, you should make your presence known.

Expanding Your Brand

Knowing how to make video content is a must-have when it comes to social media marketing. This year, there have been a lot of predictions which state that this type of content will take around 80% of the internet traffic. This is one reason why you should learn how to create interesting content to promote yourself on

YouTube and on the different social media platforms.

We've already established how YouTube is the best possible platform out there for you to host your video content. This site has more than a billion users which means that you already have a potential audience just waiting for you to come out. However, the disadvantage of YouTube is that, because there are so many existing users hosting their own channels, it can be very challenging to stand out. You need to be able to create engaging content which will differentiate yourself from the competition.

But how will you do this? What can you do differently than other people who manage other YouTube channels? What can you do to make yourself and your brand stand out among the rest? This might seem both challenging and overwhelming at first but it's not an impossible task. Here are some helpful steps to consider:

Do a lot of brainstorming and research

Before getting started, think about the main reasons why people watch videos on YouTube. Most of them want to get entertained while others want to learn new things. Think about what area you're comfortable with or which one suits your own brand and once you've made the decision, you're one step closer to your goal.

No matter what your goal is, you have to do a lot of research, especially about what the competition is doing right now. After finding more about your competition, it's time to think about how you can be better than them. How can you differentiate yourself? What do they lack? Can you do more than what they're doing? Since you're the beginner, it's your task to learn about the competition as well as any current trends which you can use for your own channel.

After researching, think about your vision. You should have a very clear picture of what you want your channel to be all about so you can find the best audience for it. With a specific identity for your brand in your mind, you can start building your channel's profile around it. No matter what type of video content you want to produce, it must add value to all of your viewers. After your viewers watch your videos, they should feel like they either learned something new or that they were entertained by the content. You should always keep your viewers in mind when you're producing videos if you want to promote yourself and your brand.

Share your video content

After creating your videos, it's time to share them. But don't do that before you've created your channel and explained what it will be all about. We've gone through the steps of creating your own channel on YouTube and by this time, you should be ready to start uploading your content and sharing it with the world.

To start off, you can invite your family, relatives, and friends to watch your videos and subscribe to your channel. It's always a good idea to start sharing with the people you're closest to because they will surely be willing to spread the word about how awesome your channel is. Then create your own email campaign and send invites to everyone on your contact list. Invite them to view your videos and if they see what they like, encourage them to subscribe to your channel. The next step would be to share your video content across other social media platforms and again, encourage everyone who views your videos to subscribe. Finally, it would also be very helpful to find some popular Facebook groups connected or relevant to the content you're producing then share your videos to those groups too. This will let others know that you exist and that they should be watching your videos.

Practice proper social media etiquette

If you want to succeed, there are certain things you must do and certain things you must avoid. For one, when you're sharing your video content, never spam your potential viewers. Think about all of the information you plan to share and provide a clear explanation of how watching your videos will be beneficial to them.

Also, one of the most important aspects of creating your own video platform is to find the best possible structure for your videos. No matter what type of videos you make, you must always follow a basic format. First, introduce the video, then give an analysis of your main topic, and before you end the video, give your audiences an effective call to action. When said at the right moment, you will notice that each time someone views your content, they end up subscribing to your channel too and this will help with the growth of your personal brand.

Finally, you have to maintain consistency and we cannot stress this enough. Without consistency, viewers won't really feel compelled to stick with you. Maybe even those who have already subscribed to your channel will end up forgetting all about you because there are other channels out there which provide a constant stream of entertaining and relevant content. By uploading videos all the time, you're creating a habit for your followers which, in turn, pushes them to keep coming back for more. It's sort of an addiction but in a good way.

Optimize to increase watch time

Right after you've posted content on YouTube, make sure to optimize it. This is an important step so that viewers can easily find your videos on YouTube and on Google search. To do this, you have to come up with the best keywords for your video. Also, you need to create a title for your video which includes powerful keywords. After you've found this perfect set of words, include them in the description and the tag of your video. This will make your content even more popular.

When creating, growing, and scaling your channel, you can look at it as your own space to be creative. Therefore, your channel should represent your style, your brand or your business. People will feel more encouraged to subscribe to channels which have consistency all throughout. This is because it shows the viewers that you don't just care about your content but also about how people see you whenever they visit your channel.

In doing all this and more (which we will discuss further in the other chapters), you will be able to increase the viewing time of your videos. There's really no point in creating videos which people will only watch for a couple of seconds then move on. The goal is for your viewers to watch the videos you publish all the way to the end. And if these videos are part of a playlist, then your viewers might want to continue watching until they've seen all that you have created. Then when they're already hooked, it's time for you to swoop in and create more compelling videos for them to enjoy.

Starting a YouTube Channel for Your Business

With enough research, persistence, and great strategies, being a famous YouTuber can also be a very lucrative business. You can make a lot of money by linking your own endorsements with brands. As a matter of fact, there are plenty of strategies you can employ to make yourself famous and earn some income through your channel. But the biggest challenge for you to face is to be able to grow an audience big enough and sustain that audience for a long time. Although it's not the easiest thing to do, creating a profitable channel on YouTube is totally possible. If this is one of your goals, keep these important tips in mind:

Know your target audience and always stay on top of the trends

As you start your channel on YouTube and to promote yourself or your brand, you should have a good idea of your target audience. This is because you would have to interact consistently with all of your viewers for as long as you want to stay on top. Without this interaction, your viewers won't feel invested in you and might not stick around to see what more you have to offer.

Unpredictability is a huge factor on YouTube too. If you don't know who your audience is, you will have a very hard time thinking about video content to share on your channel. On the other hand, if you know your audience well, then you can better predict what they want and produce the content for them.

This means that you always have to stay on top of the trends too. Even though you know your audience, if you don't know what's trending right now, you won't be able to keep up with the competition. With everything available online, people are always looking for new ideas and new videos to watch. Since you want to achieve fame, it's your job to keep producing new, innovative, creative, and interesting content to keep your audiences loyal to your channel.

Put in a lot of effort and time

Especially at the beginning, you need to focus on building your channel, growing it, and scaling it. Since there is a lot of competition out there, you really need to put in a lot of effort and time if you want to become the next YouTube star. As a matter of fact, some of the most famous YouTubers out there had to take a break from their existing commitments so that they could focus more on their channel.

Think about it, a simple video which lasts for just 3 minutes might take as long as 5 days to produce! This is especially true if you're a beginner. From shooting, splicing, and refining the video, there's a lot to do. Of course, as time goes by, you'll get better at this but when you're just starting, it would take a lot of time. And when starting your channel, you have to come up with video content regularly to keep your viewers loyal to your channel. So how would you do that if you don't put all of your energy into this venture?

Avoid using too much marketing language

Viewers prefer video content which is authentic. So if you create videos which use too much advertising or marketing language, this might end up putting them off. When people watch videos on YouTube, they want to feel entertained or enriched. They don't want to feel like they're watching an advertisement. If that were the case, they would watch television or shopping channels. This is even more undesirable if your video or channel description talks about entertainment or educational videos. Even if you have a business channel, it would be better to make content which is more about your product, how to use it in the real world, how people will benefit from it, and such without being too "corporate."

Don't be afraid to try new things

Even though your channel has an overall theme, you don't have to stick with it. Even within that theme, you can experiment and try to think of creative topics. Mixing things up once in a while will throw your viewers off in a good way and make them feel even more excited to tune in to your channel and see what else you'll come up with.

Find long-term partners who can help you with your journey

If you plan to accept sponsorships, make sure that these are in line with yourself and with your brand. When it comes to partnerships, it's always better to think in the long-term and make sure that you're only dealing with reputable, trusted retailers who won't ever rip you off.

Reaching Different Types of Audiences

Statistics show that billions of people all over the world watch videos on YouTube each day and this year, those numbers are about to grow bigger. With this in mind, you can see how important it is to start your own channel as soon as possible, especially if your goal is to explode in popularity this 2019. You have to be able to reach different types of audiences, not just the specific group that you're targeting. Here are some hard-hitting strategies which may help you achieve this goal:

Keep track of "attention score"

Great storytelling is one of the most important and irreplaceable aspects of YouTube videos. If you cannot tell a good story, you won't be able to keep audiences hooked. If you want to know how well you're doing, you can go to your dashboard and check your "attention score." This refers to the attention level of viewers and how much time they spend watching your video content. If you have a solid red score, this means you're doing relatively well. But if you see your score dropping in a specific area, you may have to make changes there.

We've talked about how there are two main types of videos which are entertainment and educational. If you're planning to make entertainment videos, here are some tips to reach a lot of audiences:

- Make sure that your video is so entertaining that it will hook your audiences within the first five seconds.

- Learn how to weave compelling stories and this will keep your viewers watching all the way to the end.

- Keep the videos short and sweet as entertainment videos aren't meant to be too lengthy.

On the other hand, if you're creating educational videos and you want to reach a wide range of audiences, here are some tips:

- Just like with entertainment videos, make sure to hook your audiences early on. When it comes to educational videos, viewers make a quick decision on whether or not they want to learn from your content.

- When teaching something to your audiences, it would be very helpful to provide systematic steps for them to accomplish what they want to learn.

- For educational videos, the length doesn't matter as much. As long as you give all of the information needed by the viewers, they will keep watching your videos all the way through.

Make use of annotations

YouTube annotations are notes which appear on your videos. You can use these to help grow your audiences through these clever techniques:

- Create a sticky note which encourages viewers to subscribe to your YouTube channel.

- Create a spotlight annotation which your viewers can click so they can go to a product or landing page.

- Create a link to related videos which is either on your channel or on one of your partner's channels.

Follow steps when planning your videos

Providing systemic steps for your audiences will keep them captivated because these steps work wonders. So why not use them for your planning too? Here are some strategic steps to guide you:

- Do a lot of keyword research for each of your videos.

- If you made use of a transcript while recording your video, upload it on the site too. This will help out a lot when people search for your video content.

- Share your videos across the different bookmarking sites such as StumbleUpon and Delicious.

- Interact with viewers and audiences on different social media networks. Share your videos, respond to comments, and answer questions that any of your subscribers and followers have.

- After some time has passed, embed your most recent video on your own blog (if you have one). This will help it get shared and spread again and again.

If you have a blog, add a YouTube widget on it

A lot of the most famous YouTubers have their own blogs too. So you may want to think about creating your own blog as well if you don't have one already. Then add a YouTube widget on your blog which can help you get more traffic on your channel. To do this, here are some steps:

- Embedding your video content on your own blog keeps the visitors on your site engaged instead of driving away the traffic.

- Make use of a Subscription Widget which asks the visitors of your blog to subscribe to your channel.

- Also, add a "call-to-action" graphic which appears while your video plays.

Add some featured channels

Another way for you to reach more audiences is to partner up with other creators of content on the site. You can easily do this by going to the page of your YouTube channel. Just make sure that the creators you partner up with are producing content in the same industry as yours and may even help highlight your own channel. After you've found these other YouTube creators, make sure to add them to your "Featured channels." The more famous you become, the more YouTube creators will make your channel one of their featured channels.

The Best Ways to Promote Your YouTube Channel

Promoting yourself is another essential part of being a YouTube star in 2019. No matter how amazing you think you are and how great your content is, if you don't promote yourself or your brand, you won't be reaching your full potential. Also, promotions will help you reach a wider audience which, in turn, will help you become more and more famous in different communities. Let's take a look at some smart strategies you can employ to promote your YouTube channel.

Build excitement among viewers by cross-promoting videos and teasers

Even if you're just starting your channel, you can build excitement through your fan base. If you have a loyal following of fans on other social media networks, then they will probably want to subscribe to your YouTube channel and become your loyal fans there too. That is if you introduce your videos in the best way possible. For instance, you can post a seemingly non-descript mood board graphic which will generate just enough interest for your viewers to want more. Make sure that this graphic will speak to your audiences and make them feel intrigued by what you have to offer.

Think of eye-catching and interesting titles for your video content

When you're trying to think of titles for your content, you need to think about what will be the most eye-catching and interesting for those who are searching for videos to watch. Remember that the first thing the viewers will see is the title of your videos so make sure it counts. It should be short, direct to the point, descriptive, and it should contain the right keywords.

Optimize your channel and your video content for SEO

If you want your channel or your videos to be found by viewers who are searching, make sure to optimize them for SEO or search engine optimization. As aforementioned, YouTube is the second biggest search engine on the internet after Google. So optimizing for SEO will guarantee that your channel or videos will show up when people search for any related content.

Work on your video thumbnails

The size of video thumbnails on YouTube mustn't exceed 2 MB. Also, the recommended resolution to use is 1280 x 720. Although the thumbnails are small, they are one of the biggest aspects you should focus on when promoting your videos on other social media networks. Think about it, your video thumbnail won't just appear on your homepage but it will also appear when people share your video or when people search for related content. When you're coming up with a design for your video thumbnail, keep these tips in mind:

- When describing your video, use a text that's clear and simple.

- If you have one, make sure to embed your logo in one of the corners of the thumbnail.

- Use bright or complementary colors when designing your thumbnail.

- Maintain consistency when making the design. As much as possible, use the same color schemes, font types, and general layout for all your video thumbnails.

Host some cool and fun contests

Everyone loves to join contests no matter where they are hosted. If you're able to think about a cool contest and you host it effectively, this will provide you with tons of cross-promotions. Hopefully, the contest will also bring to your channel a lot of new fans and subscribers. To start your contest off, produce a video with a powerful call-to-action with an announcement of the contest. Then upload the video along with the rules and a general description of the contest. Encourage the viewers to create their own entries and share the video to reach different audiences. Hosting a contest is an excellent way for you to promote yourself. In fact, those who will join your contest will do a lot of the promotions too.

Consider the analytics

Analytics are also an important part of YouTube channels. Check your analytics on YouTube as well as on the other social media networks you engage in. By examining the analytics, you can determine the times of the week when your subscribers, viewers, and fans are most active; the time of day when they are most engaged; what type of content receives the most traction; and so on. Knowing your analytics is essential if you want to successfully promote yourself on YouTube for a long time.

Don't be afraid to be different!

Finally, make sure you stand out among the rest. Remember that there are so many YouTube channels existing on YouTube right now. So standing out is actually a requirement if you want to become famous in 2019. Simple as this may seem, a lot of people feel apprehensive when it comes to being unconventional. But as soon as you get over that fear, you will surely captivate audiences from all over the world.

Chapter 7: YouTube SEO Basics

SEO stands for "Search Engine Optimization," and it's a common term in social media marketing. This refers to online search engines that we all use. A lot of people have a good understanding of how the search algorithm of Google works. After all, this is the largest search engine on the internet and virtually everyone who is online uses it. When you need to find something on Google, all you have to do is type in some keywords, click search and Google will do the work for you.

Any YouTube user knows that the site works in a similar way. Because of this, there's a very good chance that a lot of your existing or potential subscribers are performing searches using terms or keywords which are directly related to what your channel is all about on YouTube. So if you can create content which captures the attention of these people performing the searches, you will notice that you're able to reach more audiences. Learning all about YouTube SEO can help you achieve this so let's get right on it.

What You Need to Know About YouTube SEO

If you want to become famous on YouTube, it's important for you to learn all about YouTube SEO. This is invaluable information which will help boost your channel's web traffic. We've mentioned how YouTube is the second biggest online search engine so optimizing your channel is key if you want to reach a lot of people and gain a lot of new audiences. Here are some basic concepts to remember when it comes to YouTube SEO:

Keywords are vital

Marketing your channel through SEO starts with keywords. So you need to do a lot of research in order to find the best words or phrases for your content. Select keywords which are relevant to your video content and commonly searched for each month. And finally, look for related keywords which are more than just a single word in length.

Think strategically with the descriptions and titles of your video content

The descriptions and titles of your videos are very important because these are the ones which will show up when users perform searches. If you don't compose these well, the viewers won't get to see your video content.

Search for tags which work and use them

Tags are also vital when it comes to your YouTube content ranking. The good news is that you can use tags which are already popular and which are already being used by your competition. This step requires some research too but when done well, all your efforts will pay off in the end.

How YouTube Videos are Ranked Through YouTube SEO

YouTube videos are ranked on the site based on YouTube SEO. This is why it's so important to learn all about keywords and YouTube SEO. The best channels on YouTube which have achieved top rankings have users behind them who have extensive knowledge of this subject. Basically, the process of YouTube SEO involves certain steps:

YouTube SEO keyword research

When it comes to YouTube SEO, keywords are truly the most important thing. That's why the very first step to take is to research the best keywords for your video content. You can start by thinking of some keyword ideas on your own. Then you can use the YouTube feature known as Search Suggest to check if the keywords you've thought of are any good. Then you can watch videos on other channels which are similar to the ones you're planning to produce. If you see that those videos have great keywords which are already optimized, you can copy some of them for your own content.

After you've come up with a long list of potential keywords of your own and from your research efforts, it's time to select the best ones. In particular, you should choose the keywords which have low-competition, especially if you're just starting out. Otherwise, if you use high-competition keywords, viewers might not even get to see your content when they perform a search.

Publishing high-retention videos

The next step to do if you want your videos to achieve high rankings on YouTube is to make sure that the viewers will keep on watching. Audience retention refers to how many of your videos viewers watch and how long they watch your videos. This is a major ranking factor on YouTube. Simply put, if people keep on watching your videos on YouTube, your video content will move higher and higher in the ranking. To do this, make sure that:

- your videos are compelling and provide real value to the viewers

- your videos are so enjoyable that viewers will leave comments about how amazing your videos are

- your videos are so interesting that anyone who views them would subscribe to your channel

- you pay attention to your "click-through-rate" or CTR which improves when you create compelling video titles, descriptions, and thumbnails

- your videos have just the right length which would depend on what they are about

Optimizing your YouTube videos

We've already talked about optimization and we will keep on talking about it in different ways because this is hugely important for anyone who wants to become the next YouTube star. Here are some great ways to optimize your content for YouTube SEO:

- Say your most important keywords somewhere in your video for YouTube to "hear" it.

- Come up with titles for your videos which have at least 5 significant words or more.

- When creating the description of your videos, make sure to mention your keyword in the first 20-25 words then about 3 or 4 times more in the rest of the description.

- Remember that tags can be very helpful, so make sure to make them a part of all your YouTube content.

Promoting your videos

Finally, make sure that you promote yourself,

your brand, your channel, and your videos well. Do this across all of your social media networks to ensure that different types of audiences learn about you. Self-promotion is truly important and it will be very helpful in your quest to becoming famous.

Important Considerations for YouTube SEO

Right now, SEO for Google is becoming more and more popular. But if your goal is to become well-known on YouTube, the best thing you can do is use YouTube SEO as this will help you reach more people and gain more audiences. After you've created your video content for YouTube, it's time to apply SEO to it. The two important factors which affect YouTube ranking are the Video Content and User Engagement. These two make up most of YouTube SEO. In reality, there are some differences in how the search engine of YouTube works compares to the search engine of Google.

The main difference is that the search engine of YouTube can't directly determine if your target keywords are inside your video. This is why you have to say those keywords somewhere in your videos. If you don't, then the search engine isn't able to tell directly if your videos have any relevance to the tags you have used. So what does the search engine of YouTube use? It uses "video content factors" which include:

Title

This is the most important factor of YouTube SEO because it has a direct impact on your videos' CTR. So you should use the right keywords in your title while making sure that it's relevant and it accurately describes the content of your videos.

Descriptions

The main purpose of your video descriptions is to help increase your CTR since those who are searching will see exactly what your videos are all about. Then when they realize that the description matches what they're searching for, they will click on your video.

Tags

Ideally, you should use at least 10 different tags for your video. When creating these tags, make sure they're all significant to your videos. You can also use hashtags in your videos to make searching for them a lot easier. Tags and hashtags are especially useful if you're trying to start a marketing campaign or you want your videos to show up in related searches.

Transcription

You might not know this but when you upload a video, YouTube transcribes it automatically. This means that it generates a written record of your entire video for you. The reason YouTube does this is that it indexes all of the transcriptions and uses them to rank uploaded videos. This is another important reason why you should mention the main keywords in your video.

The downside is, YouTube isn't very accurate when it comes to these transcriptions. So you may have to put in some extra effort to fix the transcription made by YouTube then upload the edited text file to your original video. This will make a huge impact in your efforts in improving your YouTube SEO.

Channel Authority

In terms of your YouTube channel, you're completely in control of the content. This means how you optimize your videos; how frequently you publish content; the relevance of your titles, descriptions, and tags; how you promote your channel, and more. Therefore, you need to take very good care of your channel and keep on promoting it as this will have an effect on each of the rankings of your YouTube videos.

Content Delivery

How you deliver your content also plays a huge role in YouTube SEO. Well-delivered content makes videos more compelling, relatable, educational, entertaining, and more. By contrast, a poorly made video won't get a lot of like which, in turn, sends a negative signal that ends up lowering your ranking as time goes by. So make sure that you're always producing awesome videos and work from there.

Content Length

A lot of the best videos on YouTube are only 4 to 6 minutes in length. A lot of discussion-type and informative videos have emerged recently and these have shown how user preferences have become more and more varied. Most of the time though, users only look for relevant videos which are worth the time they spend watching. So you should always consider your time management when creating videos. Content which is either too short or too long might negatively affect the way the viewers react.

Apart from these video content factors, YouTube SEO also involves a number of "User Engagement Factors" which are:

Views

Of course, the main reason why you upload videos is so people can view them. And each time a person views your videos, this helps with your YouTube SEO. The best way to increase the views on your channel is by promoting your videos! It's even better if all the viewers watch your videos all the way to the end as this increases your videos' retention rate.

Inbound Links

YouTube also makes use of Inbound Links as one of the ranking factors for YouTube SEO. This means that you have to create links to your videos as well as your channel if you want them to achieve high rankings. In order to build these Inbound Links, you have to, again, create amazing content which is highly appealing to your viewers' emotional triggers. Then link your video to sites such as Yahoo Answers and Quora which may help increase your views and give your credibility a boost too. Linking to other sites and social networks will help you out immensely towards reaching your goals.

Social Shares

Share your links on your personal social media profiles too so all of your followers can follow suit to make your videos more and more popular.

Embeds

The purpose of this function is to bring your videos outside of YouTube's bounds. Still, YouTube can monitor all the times when your video gets embedded on different sites. This serves as a positive sign of User Engagement which, in turn, gives your YouTube SEO a boost.

Commenting and Responding to Comments

Finally, these are the most powerful factors of User Engagement in YouTube SEO. When users comment on your videos and you respond to them, this makes your content highly relevant. Be careful though because YouTube can determine which of the comments are authentic and which ones are nothing but spam. So don't even try to cheat the system. Instead, genuinely interact with your viewers and subscribers by responding to their comments. This generates more interest in your videos as it shows that you're an active YouTuber and you're not afraid to reach out to the people watching your videos.

User Reactions

These can include likes, thumbs downs, and adding your video to their favorites. Ideally, you want all of your videos to get likes and favorites instead of thumbs down reactions. The more of these you get, the higher your ranking will be on YouTube SEO. So after encouraging viewers to watch your videos and subscribe to your channel, ask them to like your videos too and maybe add these videos to their list of favorites.

Chapter 8: How FB Ads Can Help Your YouTube Channel Explode!

A lot of savvy internet users don't think Facebook Ads are too useful because no one really clicks on them. But the truth is, Facebook makes billions of dollars in revenue just from advertising. Although a lot of marketers who have tried using FB Ads stopped because for them, these "don't work," you don't have to believe them right away. The fact is, FB Ads can help you out a lot in your quest of gaining YouTube fame.

There are different types of FB Ads to choose from. These include promoting your channel, posting on your channel or your pages, and more. Despite the increasing concentration of the native FB Ads and them wanting to keep most of the internet traffic on the site, you can still find success in using FB Ads to let people know about your channel. FB Ads target users based on the information on their profile, their demographic, and their location. And a lot of unique advertising options are only available on FB. After you've created an ad, assign a budget to it then bid for every thousand impressions or click that it will receive.

The Magic of FB Ads

The great thing about Facebook is that it's providing businesses and individual users a lot of selective advertising options for their videos. For instance, FB now allows advertising on premium video content via its In-Stream Reserve program. The FB-selected content will appear to target groups only. The categories of the In-Stream Reserve program allows you to select which topics your ads will run on. Because of this, around 70% of the In-Stream video advertisements are watched all the way to the end. FB also allows advertisers a choice to advertise on one show exclusively or to advertise on several specific shows. Also, it has a ThruPlay program which only charges the advertisers whenever their videos are viewed for 15 seconds or more or if they're viewed all the way to the end.

Using FB Ads to Share Your YouTube Channel

When you use FB Ads, you can improve your channel targeting as well as gather more audiences. So if you want to target a specific group of people, using FB Ads would be highly beneficial for you. Through these ads, you can get a lot of engagement from your ideal audiences.

Just like YouTube SEO, there are some FB Advertising Optimization Techniques you can employ. When it comes to YouTube Ads, there isn't much of a level playing field. Targeting audiences isn't too specific which is why results tend to be very similar. Simply put, the time and effort you put into optimizing your YouTube Ads aren't really worth it unless you're planning to run a large campaign. Because of the inexact targeting, optimization might not be too helpful. On the other hand, if you use FB Ads, you might have a better chance of achieving the results you desire.

The Benefits of Using FB Ads to Grow Your YouTube Channel

Although technically, Facebook and YouTube are competitors, this doesn't mean that you can't grow your channel through Facebook. As a matter of fact, there is a number of benefits to using FB to increase your viewers and subscribers on your own YouTube channel. The basic idea of using FB Ads is to create a sort of bottleneck which will direct traffic towards your YouTube channel.

Once you've done that, you can leverage the traffic that you've brought to your channel and do all that you can to convert those viewers into subscribers. When you use this strategy, it would be like stretching the budget you've set for advertising out so you can achieve more than just one objective. By doing this, you can also create some extremely valuable assets which you can use in the future. Here are the benefits of using FB Ads to grow your YouTube channel:

Achieve a higher ranking

Using FB Ads can help improve your ranking. This is because more people become aware of your videos and your channel thanks to this type of promotion. And as you know, anything which can help give your ranking a boost is a good thing, especially if you want to achieve fame on YouTube.

Generate more audiences

Through FB Ads, you're essentially building and re-targeting audiences. As long as you create the best possible content, FB Ads can provide you with the perfect means for targeting. These ads can help you gather the right people together to create an audience who will love what you have to offer. Once they have clicked on your ad and watched your video, these people would be "primed" for your retargeting campaign. After allowing these audiences to mature for some time, then you can start testing your promotions and gaining some insights about the kind of people who watch your content and interact with your channel.

Gain more viewers and subscribers

Finally, using FB Ads will also allow you to grow your audiences and the number of views on your YouTube channel at a fairly low cost. If you've tried different types of advertising campaigns, you will discover that the ones offered by FB are a lot more affordable than the competition. This is especially true if you think about all the benefits they can provide you with.

Before you even start making FB Ads, make sure that your channel has a decent amount of high-quality, interesting content. Also, you should have other social media channels which are completely branded so you can backlink to them. Make sure that your YouTube channel receives enough TLC even before you pay for ads and campaigns. To do this, here are some tips:

Create the commercials

After you've ensured that your YouTube channel is set up for success, it's time to create commercials for the videos you're hosting on your channel. The reason you need to create these commercials is so you can post them on Facebook as ads to show those users what you have to offer.

Create an album on Facebook

After you've created some amazing commercials, create an album on your Facebook profile (either your personal one or your business profile) and populate the album with the incredible teasers you've made. Then you can start running your ads with these short but compelling commercials.

Build your audiences

Although you can skip this step and just create a traffic campaign to build your audiences, you may also want to start video view campaigns which are quite affordable. Also, the audiences you gather tend to convert better compared to when you just run them through cold traffic. For the best results, you can run both types of campaigns. Doing this will surely give your audience base a boost.

Request the viewers to subscribe to your channel

After you've launched your campaigns, you also need to include a subscription link to your ads and your videos. This is a simple process, all you have to do is add the link to the end of your YouTube channel. This will route your users to a subscription page automatically even before they finish watching the entire video.

How to Get Massive Views on Your YouTube Channel Through Facebook

If you're planning to share your YouTube videos on Facebook, the simplest way to do this is to copy the URL from your channel and paste it on Facebook. Even easier, you can just click the "share on Facebook" icon which is one of the sharing options available on the site. Some people also try uploading relevant images on FB then adding their YouTube video link in the image's description. But which of these strategies work best? To know this, it's important to learn how FB prioritizes shared or uploaded posts:

- FB gives more importance to posts which contain videos uploaded on the site directly.

- After these FB-native videos, FB gives secondary importance to posts which have images uploaded on the site directly.

- After these images, FB prioritizes posts which only contain text.

- Lastly, FB prioritizes posts which contain YouTube links.

This means that when you only post a link of your YouTube channel or videos, there's a chance that this will get suppressed in your audiences' feeds.

Therefore, it would be better if you:

- Take a screengrab or a snapshot of your video which perfectly matches the thumbnail of your video or one which is really catchy. Better yet, you can create a short teaser of your video to upload on FB.

- If you really want to make use of a YouTube URL, make sure to "disguise" it using a URL shortener. You can also use a shortener for URLs of your playlists which would improve your audience retention. This is because as soon as a person clicks on the URL to watch your video, he will discover that there are more videos with related content which he can watch one after the other.

- Create a text-only FB post and include your video or playlist's shortened URL. Then include a photo with your post and upload the photo first so that your post initially registers as an image.

Facebook and Facebook Ads are extremely useful because they increase your videos' viewability as the interaction increases. So if your post receives a lot of comments, replies, likes, and more, the more exposure it will have. This is because your post will keep on appearing on the feeds of FB viewers each time it receives likes, reactions, replies, and comments. But among all the interactions which can occur on Facebook, the one which carries the most weight in terms of promotion is "shares." That's why you should always share your post to other people right after you've uploaded it on the site.

Chapter 9: IG Ads are Highly Effective Too!

Apart from using Facebook Ads to promote your YouTube channel, you may also want to consider using Instagram Ads. Instagram Ads showcase video clips or photos with text-based messages or captions. Also, Instagram or IG is designed to be accessed by users through tablets or smartphones. Of course, you can also access the site using your desktop or laptop's web browser.

Although Facebook is the owner and operator of IG, it has maintained the site as a separate social media platform. But because of this connection, you can easily link your Facebook account to your IG account so when you post something on IG, it will automatically get published on FB right away if you want it to. To make things easier for yourself and your fans, it's best to use the same name across all of your social media accounts, even your own YouTube channel.

Since IG focuses more on publishing video clips and photos, you can use this to your advantage to promote your YouTube videos and YouTube channel. For instance, if you're trying to promote your new YouTube video, uploading a post on IG which showcases your video's thumbnail along with a text-based caption will go a long way in encouraging IG users to check out your latest content. Just make sure that your message also includes a URL address or a hyperlink of your video so anyone who's interested can go directly to your video's location.

Rather than posting your video, you can also promote your YouTube channel by including a link to your main page or to one of your best playlists. That way, anyone who clicks on the link will have access to all of your video content instead of just one video. Just like on Facebook, you can also create a short teaser clip and publish that on IG for everyone to see. If you want to generate your own following on IG to help expand your YouTube channel's audiences, you can use the site as an effective tool for sharing video content and images related to your channel. But just like any other social media network, make sure that you're always providing interesting content and you're always interacting with your followers and subscribers.

Using IG Ads to Spread the Word of Your YouTube Channel

Unless you choose the paid advertising option on IG, creating an IG account and managing it for your personal use is free of charge. The only things you need to invest on are your time and commitment to manage your account, interact with your audiences, and develop unique, interesting content regularly. Even though IG is a different social media platform from YouTube, it's important to employ a synergistic approach in terms of your branding, your account's appearance, and the messages that you want to convey. Do this so all of your accounts are in line with each other and you will always meet the needs and expectations of your audiences.

Just like YouTube, Instagram is free for everyone to use. This app allows you to freely share videos and photographs on your account for the purposes of promoting yourself. This means that using IG Ads can help you out immensely if you're trying to gain YouTube fame this 2019. The main method used to attract IG followers to your YouTube channel is the "link-in bio" strategy. IG provides you the opportunity to use one interactive connection in your personal bio. Therefore, you need to make sure that you use this opportunity well. Here are other tips for using IG Ads to spread the word of your YouTube channel:

Make use of trending hashtags to reach more audiences on Instagram

When you use multiple trending hashtags for the subtitles of your photos, this motivates users to check out the content you're promoting. You can create your own hashtags or use some which have already proven their worth. Either way, make sure that the hashtags you use are relevant to your content and will help you gain more followers.

Share your newest videos on Instagram as video teasers

Instagram allows you to have live connections in your bio. But this doesn't mean that you can't just use this to connect your most recent YouTube video. Instead, it would be better for you to use this feature to get more users to visit your IG landing page to see more of your videos and photos. This, in turn, will motivate these users to check out your YouTube channel and all the content on it. If you want to generate interest, share teasers and sneak peeks of your most recent videos.

If you want to create a lot of hype before uploading a new video on YouTube, create a teaser and post it on Instagram, Facebook, and on other social media platforms. A 15-second long video clip which highlights the best features of your new video will suffice. When done well, these will surely give those users a reason to see what you have to offer.

Interact with Instagram Influencers in your own niche

Earlier on, we talked about YouTube Influencers. These are the people who are already famous and who already have a good following. The good news is that Instagram has its own set of Influencers and a lot of them have the same followers on YouTube. If any of these Influencers in your own niche happen to start an interaction with you, make sure to interact back. For instance, if they comment on your post, make use of their usernames when replying to those comments. Also, you can go to their profiles and follow them in the hopes that they reciprocate this action. Such interactions can help IG users learn more about you and what you're all about.

Collaborate with Instagram Influencers who also do vlogging on YouTube

This is another great strategy to employ if you

want to spread the word about yourself. Connect with famous YouTube vloggers and users who have a huge influence and a huge following. Vloggers are very popular right now so even if you don't plan to publish this kind of content, collaborating with these types of users will really help you out.

Interact with all the other Instagram users too

If you want to generate interest on your IG account, make sure to maintain interactions. Gathering comments or likes requires you to start connecting with different users and followers. But before doing this, you have to understand that you can accomplish more through likes than through comments because likes are easier to do. Unless a user is really invested in your post or he found it truly remarkable, he may just end up liking your post instead of commenting on it.

Promote your videos through the site

Instagram is a more recent addition compared to

YouTube and Facebook. Still, it's quickly becoming one of the more popular social media platforms out there. IG is a highly-engaged community which has over 500 million users who are actively interacting with each other and sharing their own stories. Despite having a simple design, it offers visual inspiration to its users. This shows that IG offers a lot of potential in terms of promoting your YouTube channel and all of your video content. So you can see this site as another avenue to use when trying to spread the word of your channel.

Growing Your YouTube Audience Via IG

Although the road to becoming a YouTube sensation in 2019 can be a long and challenging one, it's not an impossible quest. As long as you commit to the task and you have a lot of time and patience, you will have a high chance of succeeding. If you want to grow your YouTube audience through IG, give these strategies a try:

Come up with "behind the scenes" videos for your viewers

One of the most authentic things you can do when you have your own YouTube channel is to bond with your fans. This is also a great way to show them how genuine you are and how vested you are in their interests. To do this, you can create "behind the scenes" videos and show them to your viewers too. Such videos are always a lot of fun to watch and your viewers will surely appreciate them.

Showcase music tracks which are also 15-seconds in length

Along with a great image, upload a sample of your most recent track on IG which is about 15-seconds in length. This is a great trick which allows you to make use of the audio capabilities of the site. If your main purpose is to create music on your YouTube channel, you can do this to generate interest among your fans.

Post shoutouts to your fans

Fans love the attention so when you post shoutouts as a reply to their comments, they will surely be loyal to you for a long time. You can use IG to shine the spotlight on your most loyal subscribers to keep their loyalty and to help them encourage others to become one of your fans.

Featuring Your YouTube Channel on IG Stories

Unlike YouTube, Instagram has a story feature wherein you can share parts of your life with all of your followers in a unique way. Through Instagram Stories, your fans can access your photos and short videos about your everyday life. This makes it easier for them to interact with you on a more personal level. Here are some ways you can use this feature to promote your YouTube channel:

Hold some exclusive contests and giveaways

This is an excellent way to encourage your

Instagram followers to watch your YouTube videos and vice versa. Hold exclusive contests and giveaways on your YouTube channels and make the announcement of winners on IG Stories. Just make sure to inform your followers when you will be making the announcement so they know when to check your IG Stories.

Make significant updates and announcements

If you want to make any significant updates and announcements about your personal life, you can share these on IG Stories. For instance, if you're creating travel vlogs, you can inform your viewers where you plan to travel next, what types of videos you're currently working on, and what you plan to create in the future. Sharing this information in IG Stories will encourage new users, viewers, and followers to learn more about your channel.

Use polls to involve your followers in any of your creative decisions

If you're stuck and you can't decide on your next video ideas, why not ask your audience to help you decide? Involving your followers when you're trying to make creative decisions will make them feel more important. Millions of users are actively engaged on IG each day and the Story feature of the site is one of the best ways for you to encourage more people to see what your channel is all about.

Effective IG Marketing Tips to Promote Your YouTube Channel

Now that you know the potential of Instagram in promoting your YouTube channel, we can go to the more practical information. In order to successfully promote your YouTube channel using Instagram, you need to follow some strategic marketing tips. These include:

- Make use of several hashtags when posting your YouTube content on Instagram. This works well on other social media platforms too.

- When thinking of hashtags, throw in a couple of the most trending hashtags which are relevant to your YouTube channel's content.

- Share a lot of unique content if you want to generate interest. Sharing content that's already been done won't encourage users to see what you're offering.

- Brand all of your posts on Instagram. Whether you're sharing photos or videos, make sure that they all fit in with your own brand whether it be personal or business-related.

- Include the details of your YouTube channel on your posts. This will make it easier for IG users to find you on YouTube, watch your videos, and subscribe to your channel.

- Always link your most recent YouTube video in your IG profile.

- Post the right kinds of updates on IG to generate interest in your YouTube channel.

- Interact with all of your IG followers. Through these interactions, you can also encourage your followers to watch your videos and subscribe to your YouTube channel.

Chapter 10: YouTube: Your Lifetime Business

All over the world, there are YouTube stars who have made their venture a lucrative business. These people have discovered how to make a lot of money through the video content that they publish on their channel. Even though these YouTube celebrities make it look easy, there is actually a lot involved. But if you're able to gain fame AND earn from your channel, you can make YouTube your lifetime business!

How YouTube Can Help You Earn Money

If you want to become famous and start earning money through your YouTube channel this 2019, now is the best time to start. The great news is that there are a lot of famous YouTubers and YouTube channels to imitate, inspire, and motivate you. The statistics are very promising too. According to YouTube, channels which are earning five figures and above has grown in number in the past few months. The same thing goes for the channels which are earning six figures yearly. You definitely want to be part of these statistics!

To become famous, you want people to get to know you better or if you want to attract sponsors, partners, and advertisers. To do this, you should also know yourself well, know what you want to do, and know who your target audience is. Set yourself up as a person who is "brand safe" so you can connect with other creators all over the world who also want to share their brand and develop content along with you. Also, there are some things you should avoid such as using profane language and talking about controversial or political topics on your YouTube channel which might turn off your audiences.

One of the best ways to earn income through your YouTube channel is through the talents you have and the ones you have developed through your personal and professional life. YouTube videos don't just earn money through ad-sharing. Some sell their products and services online, others partner with local businesses, and some even make public appearances in different events after they have already achieved superstar status.

Of course, having your own external income stream is extremely important too. No matter how popular you are, things can change in an instant which might compromise your income. So don't quit your day job just yet, especially if you're just starting out. As long as you have enough time to focus on your channel as well as your work, try to do both simultaneously to secure your financial future.

When you're starting out, think about your start-up costs. These expenses would depend on the type of video content you're planning to produce. For instance, if you plan to create a "how-to" channel, all you need are the supplies for the procedures you're going to teach. And if you already have these supplies at home, then you won't have to spend a lot of money on your first few videos. But if you want to create a gaming channel where you livestream tournaments, you may need to invest in a high-end computer so you can play the game online while broadcasting your feed to your viewers. In such case, you may have to spend a lot of money from the beginning.

If one of your videos has done really well, you may receive an email from YouTube with a subject line saying "Apply for revenue sharing for your video." Receiving such an email is an amazing opportunity. But even if your application is approved, you can only earn money from the specific video mentioned in the email you received. On the other hand, if you believe that you have a sufficient number of video uploads and video views, you can directly apply on the Partner Program page of YouTube for partnership. If your application is approved here, you have the option to turn on the "revenue sharing" feature for all of your video content. That is as long as all of your videos meet the criteria. Some people even rent their videos out to other users. It's important to note though, that if your application is rejected, you won't be able to send another application for 2 whole months.

If YouTube approves your application, you should also create your own account on Google AdSense. Then link this account to your YouTube account because this is where you will receive the payments from your videos. After applying, you also have to wait patiently because sometimes, it takes weeks for YouTube to review your videos before you get a reply. Also, YouTube will only send you payments after your videos have made a minimum of $100. But as long as you persist, you keep on creating amazing content, and you remain consistent, you may see your efforts paying off in the long-run.

Tips for Promoting Your YouTube Channel in 2019

We've already gone through the importance of promoting your YouTube channel if you want to become famous on the site. If you want to monetize your YouTube channel, you promoting it is also an important step as with any other type of social media marketing. Growing your audiences and increasing your number of subscribers will ultimately increase your chances of earning lucratively. To do this, here are some smart promotional tips to consider:

- Come up with a plan and a script for all of your individual videos. Planning includes the structure of your video content to make sure that all your videos are organized and have a smooth flow. And if you have a script to follow, this will make it easier for you when you're actually filming your videos. Just make sure that when you're composing your script, you use language that's appropriate to your audiences.

- Make sure that the videos you create are highly engaging, entertaining, and informative, and that the entire video has these qualities. Otherwise, your viewers might click on another video once they get bored with watching yours.

- Increase the frequency of uploading your videos. This is extremely important if you want to gain a lot of loyal subscribers. No matter how much your viewers love watching your videos, if you don't keep giving them content quickly, they might lose interest or worse, find another wannabe YouTuber who uploads more frequently than you do.

- Make the most of the customization features for your channel. If you want people to know right away that they've clicked on your channel or on one of your videos, you need to brand everything in a unified way. Also, making yourself look professional will make the viewers trust and respect you. Customize everything in such a way that everything you're creating is easily recognizable across all of the social media networks and platforms.

- Create a personalized thumbnail for your video as well as an engaging trailer. Creating these will surely help promote your videos and your channel, especially if you're able to do them each time you have a new video. The thumbnails and the trailers will generate interest in your content and, ultimately, in your channel too.

- Don't forget your "call-to-action" annotations. If you use these well, you can encourage more viewers to subscribe to your channel so they can see the other video content you've already produced.

- Make the most out of the available online tools. There are several tools out there which you can use to promote yourself, your channel, and your video content. From tools which can help you create better videos to tools which can help you promote those videos, there are plenty to choose from and they all have the potential to help you achieve your YouTube goals.

- Make sure that people can find you. There are many ways to do this. For instance, YouTube provides you with an option to link your channel to your personal or official page. The same thing goes for other social media networks. The more you promote yourself on different sites and platforms, the easier it will be for people to become aware of your channel.

- As much as possible, keep your videos short, entertaining, informative, simple, and less than 5 minutes. Challenging as this may be, this is also an important step, especially if you want to keep your audiences wanting for more.

- Make use of an Intro and an Outro as this

will help in your branding. These will make your videos more entertaining and it will also increase the overall feeling of professionalism.

- Keep on editing your videos until they are perfect. Unless you feel like the video you had produced is the best that you can possibly make, don't upload it yet. Do this to ensure that your viewers are only getting the best from you.

- Always conclude your videos on a positive note. This will give your viewers a good feeling each time they're done watching one of your videos. Doing this will also keep your viewers hooked on you and your content.

- Remember that promotion is more effective when you collaborate with other YouTubers. Just make sure that you choose the people you collaborate with and they don't end up becoming competitors.

- Interactions, competitions, and giveaways are also an excellent way to promote your videos and your channel. So once in a while, insert these in your regular video content line up to generate excitement and to encourage your viewers to spread the word about your channel.

In-platform promotion is very important too. This means promoting your channel within the site so you can get a lot of comments, views, and thumbs-ups from viewers. Doing this will increase the ranking of your videos which, in turn, can improve the popularity of your channel. Here are some effective in-platform promotional tips for you:

- Before uploading your videos, make sure you've optimized them already. This includes the title, the description, and the use of hashtags and keywords which will help in the promotion of your content.

- Add closed captioning and subtitles to all of your videos as this will help increase views.

- Always use a high-resolution camera when you're filming your videos to rank better.

- Apart from encouraging your viewers to subscribe, encourage them to like and leave comments on your videos too as these will improve your ranking.

- Create a combination of classic content as well as trending content to ensure long-term success.

- Make use of tools for long-tail keyword suggestions for your video descriptions and titles.

- Consider adding subtitles to your videos if you're targeting audiences from all over the world.

- If you have a blog, write posts about your

best or most popular videos on it. This will inform your followers about the content of your YouTube channel and get them interested in what you're producing.

- Watch other users' videos and leave comments on their videos too. This type of interaction can also spread the word about your own channel to others.

Different Ways You Can Make Money on YouTube

These days, there are several influencer platforms where you can try your hand at becoming famous. But among all of these, YouTube happens to be the most lucrative platform as well as the most influential one. If you're able to become famous while producing amazingly successful videos, you can start earning money on YouTube.

Where the viewers go, money usually follows. A lot of people are now focused on getting their video fix from their smartphones and other devices instead of television. This gives YouTube users the opportunity to earn a lot on the site. If you want to earn on YouTube, that doesn't entail just making videos. You should also make sure that you're constantly uploading high-quality content on your YouTube channel to build a huge fan base and audience. Also, here are the different ways you can earn money on the site:

Make money through ads

This is the simplest method to earn money on the site. But before you can do this, you need to apply as a partner on the YouTube Partner Program as we discussed in the previous section. To increase your chances of your application getting approved, you should at least have a thousand subscribers and a minimum of 4,000 hours viewed. Only after becoming a partner will you be able to make money through ads.

When it comes to earning through ads, you will receive payment based on two metrics namely the number of times the ads have been clicked and the number of times the ads have been viewed. This means that you need to make sure that your audiences will click on the ads you show on your videos and they watch the ads for at least 30 seconds. The revenue you get from this method gets divided between yourself and YouTube/Google. Basically, the site gets to keep 45% of the revenue earned which means that you get to keep the rest. This is the first method most YouTubers employ when they want to earn money on the site. If you're already earning consistently through this method (mind you, it would take some time), then you can look into the other methods.

Crowdfunding

This works best if you have an incredible idea but you don't have the funds to execute it. Crowdfunding can help you achieve your goal in such a case. Create a video which explains your idea and include an interactive card within the video which will take your viewers to the crowdfunding landing page.

Host events

This works well if you've already built a name for yourself on YouTube. Then if you want to bond with your fans, you can try hosting events. Then create a video which tells your fans about your event. Then you can sell your merchandise or tickets to your event and earn some money in the process.

License your video content

You can use this method every time one of your videos goes viral. Then you can license those videos to online news sites, morning shows, and other types of news outlets in exchange for a fee.

Rent your videos out

This works a lot like pay per view. When you rent your videos out, the renters will pay you directly. If you want to employ this method, set the rental price and create a trailer to advertise this service.

Sell your merchandise or products

Since YouTube is the second biggest search engine online, you should see it as a huge resource. So once you've achieved fame, you may try to start selling your merchandise or products on your channel. You don't have to actually "sell" these products. Instead, you will just increase the exposure of what you're selling. In a way, this will also bring you closer to your fans as they learn more about you.

For instance, if you already have an existing e-commerce storefront, this means that you already have something to sell. So you can start creating a couple of videos related to the niche of your product. Then before ending the video, introduce your shop or your product and include a link which will take the viewers to your shop's landing page. You also have the option to partner up with existing merchandising networks and promote their products and services.

Sponsorships

Most of the famous and successful YouTubers out there have advertisements and sponsorships in their video content. When it comes to sponsorships, you don't have to share your earnings with the site. Also, you can negotiate the contracts with your sponsors based on how big your audience is and on impressions.

Work with different brands

Influencer marketing is huge these days. That's why ad agencies and brands all around the globe are promoting their services and products through the most famous YouTube stars who already have a loyal following. So if you've already achieved this status, these businesses might try contacting you!

The bottom line is although earning money on YouTube can be a long and challenging process, it's not impossible. As long as you put in the time, patience, and effort, you will see all of this pay off in the end.

Conclusion: Youtube: The New Frontier

Officially, social media platforms have started back in the year 1997 wherein the very first large-scale social media network was known as "Six Degrees." Since then, there had been numerous attempts at creating such platforms but only a few of them succeeded. History has provided us with some incredible examples of successful social media networks but among all of them, only one stood out. That is if you look at the definition of "success" as having a thriving ecosystem where content creators, users, brands, and more all benefit from using the platform. Based on this definition, we can say that since the beginning, the most successful social media platform that ever existed has been YouTube and it's still around until now.

Of course, this doesn't mean that the other social media platforms haven't gained their own successes. Facebook, Instagram, Snapchat, and all the others out there have enjoyed a lot of success too, especially in this modern world where we all rely on our smartphones and gadgets to communicate with each other and keep up with the latest news. But as we've said, YouTube stands out among the rest because it has features that all these other social media channels don't possess. Here are some of the main reasons why YouTube is the "most successful" platform for social media now:

The content creators on YouTube can earn through the site

This is one of the main reasons why content creators keep coming up with new content for the users to view. Since they can earn from the content they're uploading, they're properly motivated to keep on producing and uploading videos on their channels. Right now, other social media platforms such as Facebook and Instagram don't provide opportunities to earn money directly through their account. Rather, the users have to collaborate with third parties if they want to get paid.

Without the potential to earn or any other kind of incentive, the creators won't feel too motivated to post consistently on the platform. Either that or they will post content which isn't compelling or of high-quality. Without amazing content to look out for, the users won't stick around for too long. And when the users stop visiting the site, the brands and advertisers will leave too. Eventually, the site will start failing because nobody is using it anymore.

The compensation received by creators drives them to do better and it also helps strengthen their loyalty to YouTube. Furthermore, it gives the creators the resources to improve their video production which, in turn, helps them come up with even better content. Also, the opportunity to earn provides the channel creators with a healthy dose of competition by giving even the new creators a reason to strive more.

Of course, compensation doesn't always have to

come in the form of money. It can also come in the form of becoming a celebrity, getting in touch with the top professionals in the industry, networking opportunities, and so much more. But this compensation given to the channel creators doesn't just come from nothing, especially the monetary compensation. Sometimes, companies acquire their funding internally before they shell it out to the creators.

It has a unique kind of community

Again, the compensation factor also plays a huge role in building a motivated community on any social media platform. On YouTube, the creators who possess their own channels and earn from the video content they upload are considered as professionals. These people are an important part of something even bigger than themselves individually. The YouTube stars and the other YouTube earners are actually running the site and taking care of it. In return, the site takes great care of them too.

The longer you stay on YouTube, the more your natural human tendencies will start kicking in. You will get to know other creators (especially if you collaborate with them) and eventually, you will be part of a unique type of community. When you look at YouTube from the perspective of the users, the community is almost exclusively run by the YouTube creators which makes the job of YouTube much easier. Any platform which has millions of loyal and dedicated users who will watch the video content published by the creators and purchase what they're selling, the community, for the most part, cares for itself.

It mobilizes talent which is not represented well

The fact is, the other social media platforms out there will never possess the creative power that YouTube possesses. And this is mainly because these other platforms don't directly pay their influencers and they don't have any kinds of standalone products for the users to create content on. Take Facebook, for example. It does provide a lot of content but all of the content comes from third parties all around the internet.

YouTube is a place where talented individuals who don't have proper representation can make themselves known to the world. A lot of aspiring filmmakers who, unfortunately, don't have a lot of connections in the industry can share their work for others to see. YouTube is the perfect avenue to mobilize talented individuals to grow a platform that's full of creative content. This is another thing that sets the site apart from the other social media networks on the internet now. The creative users uploading content on the site keep it thriving. Without these creative individuals, YouTube won't survive and nobody will be interested in investing their brands and businesses in the channel.

It provides recognition and gamification

This is another excellent reason why YouTube stands out. Right now, YouTube offers 3 awards to the creators who reach specific milestones:

- If you gather 100,000 subscribers on your channel, you will receive a Silver Play Button

- If you gather a million subscribers on your channel, you will receive a Gold Play Button

- If you gather 10 million subscribers on your channel, you will receive a Diamond Play Button

Because of this, consistently making use of the site becomes a lot more fun. Receiving rewards for all the effort and hard work they put into their content keeps the creators loyal and inspired. And when these creators keep uploading compelling videos, it keeps the users coming back for more.

It provides welcome competition

Just like any other business, social media platforms should offer a healthy amount of competition if they want to facilitate a thriving ecosystem. Since there are thousands of YouTube channel creators out there, they are constantly competing with each other to gain the most number of subscribers. This is one of the reasons why these users keep trying to come up with creative content so they can stand out. And this creative competition is highly beneficial for the users because they're the ones who enjoy all of the content being created by the creators. So it's definitely a win-win situation which, again, sets YouTube apart from all the rest.

YouTube Monetization

YouTube monetization seems like a great way to generate income but it's not as easy as it sounds. Unless you're a superstar and you're already famous even before you've started your channel, it may take some time to generate enough followers so you can start monetizing the video content you're creating. Famous as you may become, keep in mind that as a YouTuber, you won't be able to enjoy a consistent salary flow. Then you also have to deal with a number of payment hurdles on the site.

But if you really plan on monetizing your YouTube channel, there are some things you need to know. First of all, the website has several rules which are meant to regulate those who can and can't make money on the site. These rules only apply to advertising but they may also have an effect on the number of people who can watch your videos and if the viewers click on your videos. Here are some rules for you to keep in mind while you plan to monetize your YouTube channel:

- Your content has to be advertiser-friendly.

- Your content is original or you've obtained permission to use the content for commercial purposes.

- You can provide official documentation which proves that you own the commercial rights to all of your video and audio content.

- The content you produce complies with all the policies of the YouTube Partner Program, the site's Terms of Service, and the Community Guidelines.

Also, keep in mind that if you don't follow any of these guidelines, YouTube has the right to disable monetization for your account. The YouTube Partner Program is an important aspect of YouTube Monetization. This program is in charge of controlling and keeping track of all of YouTube's advertising applicants. So if you want to monetize your channel or the content you're creating, the first thing you need to do is apply for this program. To do this, you must have at least 4,000 viewing hours in the past year along with a thousand subscribers to your channel.

Technically, YouTube doesn't pay you directly. Rather, you get your monetary compensation from Google Adsense. Adsense aggregates all of your views then it deposits funds to your account each month. The reality is, YouTubers don't really make a lot of money when you look at the basic pay rate. But if you keep on creating awesome content and you gain more and more viewers, those small numbers can add up until you're earning a good amount of money each month. This is the main challenge of those who want to earn a lot on YouTube. But if you commit to the task and you have a lot of creative ideas which you know your viewers will love, then it's definitely worth a try!

Ways to Monetize Your YouTube Channel

As the internet becomes more and more popular, online media is quickly following suit. In this modern world, we now have a lot of social media platforms to choose from. Your choice would depend on what you're looking for and what you want to achieve. Basically, if you want to become famous and have the chance to earn some money, then YouTube is the platform for you.

When it comes to potential success in terms of monetary compensation, there's no other social media platform more lucrative than this one. Think about it, some of the most famous and successful vloggers have claimed that they're able to earn more than $100,000 each year! Of course, this didn't happen overnight. It took a lot of time, effort, patience, and commitment to reach this level of success.

We've already talked about the first steps you need to take in order to monetize your YouTube channel. After you've setup your Adsense account, you can set your preferences for monetization. These preferences allow you to choose which kinds of ads will be associated with your video content. You also have to verify that you want to monetize all of your current and future video content. If you're lucky enough to get approved by the YouTube Partner Program, there are different ways you can make money. The best ones are:

Using pre-roll ads

A pre-roll ad is a type of advertisement which

plays before your video plays. This type of ad makes a lot more money per thousand views compared to ads which stay on a video's sidebar. And every time a viewer clicks on the ad, you earn a profit along with a smaller amount each time it's viewed. Pre-roll ads are usually 15 seconds long or even shorter so it's not bothersome for viewers to watch. These ads serve as a quick and easy way to earn money through clicks.

Obtaining sponsors for your YouTube channel

Right now, advertisers and brands are all searching for YouTube celebrities and influencers to promote their products and services. If you've already achieved the fame you're searching for, you can try obtaining sponsors for your channel. Reach out to brands and businesses relevant to your niche and start a conversation with them. If you manage to obtain some great sponsors, make sure to inform your viewers that you're getting paid to endorse products and services so you won't risk breaking the platform bylaws of YouTube as well as the rules set by the FTC.

Cater to the subscribers of YouTube Red

YouTube Red is a type of service on the site. When users subscribe to YouTube Red, it removes any ads from their video-watching experiences. They can also enjoy a number of benefits that other YouTube users don't have access to. If you link your channel to this service, you can receive a commission based on how long the subscribers of YouTube Red stay on your channel and watch your videos. So try thinking of video content which will capture the attention of this specific demographic. As your viewers increase, you may start seeing a profit!

There are other ways to earn money on YouTube, some of which we have already discussed in the previous chapter. If you want to monetize your YouTube channel, you need to make sure that you learn all that you can about these different methods. Also, you can give these methods a try and see which one works best for yourself and your channel. Again, remember to be patient, persistent, and consistent if you want the cash to keep on flowing.

YouTube and Beyond

YouTube is one of the most powerful social media platforms existing in the online world now. This is because it's supported by amazing trends. First of all, the shifts of generational consumption never reverse. This means that people who have shifted to YouTube (and other social media platforms) from television aren't likely to go back. They've already seen what YouTube has to offer and it's far more diverse and exciting than anything else that's available out there.

Then there's the global reach of the site. For the first time in history, billions of people from all around the world can watch the same video content simultaneously. The best part is, different types of videos can go viral. So even if you create content using a very limited budget, as long as it's compelling to different audiences, it can reach those billions of people who are already tuned into the site.

No matter how you look at it, YouTube is a huge part of 2019 and of the future. If you want to become famous on the site and start monetizing your channel, there's no better time than today. With all of the information you have learned and all of the information that's available online, you can start your own channel, share your talents, and begin your journey to YouTube fame.

References

Balkhi, S. (2019). *5 Video Marketing Trends You Should Follow in 2019*. [online] Entrepreneur. Available at: https://www.entrepreneur.com/article/324554 [Accessed 2 Feb. 2019].

Bullas, J. (2019). *3 Reasons Why YouTube Videos go Viral*. [online] Jeffbullas's Blog. Available at: https://www.jeffbullas.com/3-reasons-why-youtube-videos-go-viral/ [Accessed 2 Feb. 2019].

Feldman, B. (2019). *YouTube: What Is It and Why Use It? » Tech Tips » Surfnetkids*. [online] Tech Tips » Surfnetkids. Available at: https://www.surfnetkids.com/tech/1200/youtube-what-is-it-and-why-use-it/ [Accessed 2 Feb. 2019].

HuffPost. (2019). *7 Astonishing Facts About YouTube That You've Never Heard*. [online] Available at:

https://www.huffingtonpost.com/kathleen-maloney/7-astonishing-facts-about_b_14630278.html [Accessed 2 Feb. 2019].

iMore. (2019). *YouTube: Everything you need to know!.* [online] Available at: https://www.imore.com/youtube-everything-you-need-know [Accessed 2 Feb. 2019].

Investopedia. (2019). *How Do People Make Money on YouTube?.* [online] Available at: https://www.investopedia.com/ask/answers/012015/how-do-people-make-money-videos-they-upload-youtube.asp [Accessed 2 Feb. 2019].

Justin Bryant I'm an entrepreneur, s. (2019). *7 YouTube Trends and Algorithm Changes for the Future (2018 and 2019) - Self Made Success.* [online] Self Made Success. Available at: http://selfmadesuccess.com/youtube-trends/ [Accessed 2 Feb. 2019].

Lifewire. (2019). *YouTube 101: What Beginners Need to Know About Using YouTube.* [online] Available at: https://www.lifewire.com/youtube-

101-3481847 [Accessed 2 Feb. 2019].

me, m., Together, L., 1:1, W., U, J., Rockstars, J., up, h., Planners, D. and TRAINING!, F. (2019). *Basics of Starting a YouTube Channel | Hey Jessica*. [online] Hey Jessica. Available at: http://jessicastansberry.com/basics-of-youtube/ [Accessed 2 Feb. 2019].

ReelnReel. (2019). *YouTube Trends And Predictions For 2019 | ReelnReel*. [online] Available at: https://www.reelnreel.com/youtube-trends-and-predictions-for-2019/ [Accessed 2 Feb. 2019].

The Odyssey Online. (2019). *Why YouTube Is So Successful*. [online] Available at: https://www.theodysseyonline.com/youtube-successful [Accessed 2 Feb. 2019].

ValueWalk. (2019). *YouTube Influencer Marketing Trends For 2019: What You Need To Know*. [online] Available at: https://www.valuewalk.com/2018/12/youtube-influencer-marketing/ [Accessed 2 Feb. 2019].

Video Production by Invisible Harness. (2019). *Understanding YouTube and it's purpose for Marketing.* [online] Available at: http://www.invisibleharness.com/understanding-youtube-purpose/ [Accessed 2 Feb. 2019].

Webwise.ie. (2019). *Explained: What is YouTube?.* [online] Available at: https://www.webwise.ie/parents/what-is-youtube/ [Accessed 2 Feb. 2019].

Yarbrough, R. and Yarbrough, R. (2019). *YouTube Marketing in 2019: Future Video Marketing Trends and Tips – Feedster.* [online] Feedster. Available at: https://www.feedster.com/at-work/social-media/social-media-marketing/youtube/youtube-marketing-in-2019/ [Accessed 2 Feb. 2019].

Buffer Marketing Library. (2019). *How to Create a YouTube Channel in 3 Simple Steps.* [online] Available at: https://buffer.com/library/create-a-youtube-channel [Accessed 2 Feb. 2019].

Convince and Convert: Social Media Consulting and Content Marketing Consulting. (2019). *How to Make a Successful YouTube Channel*. [online] Available at: https://www.convinceandconvert.com/social-media-strategy/how-to-make-a-successful-youtube-channel/ [Accessed 2 Feb. 2019].

Forbes.com. (2019). *7 Reasons To Start A YouTube Channel Now (And First Steps To Take)*. [online] Available at: https://www.forbes.com/sites/jaysondemers/2018/05/30/7-reasons-to-start-a-youtube-channel-now-and-first-steps-to-take/#309e60f26a04 [Accessed 2 Feb. 2019].

Harven, M. (2019). *What YouTube is Doing for Education |*. [online] EdTech Times. Available at: https://edtechtimes.com/2015/01/07/youtube-education/ [Accessed 2 Feb. 2019].

Influencer Marketing Hub. (2019). *12 Best Types of YouTube Content To Succeed at Growing a YouTube Channel*. [online] Available at:

https://influencermarketinghub.com/12-best-types-of-youtube-content/ [Accessed 2 Feb. 2019].

Lifewire. (2019). *What Is a YouTube Channel?*. [online] Available at: https://www.lifewire.com/channel-youtube-1616635 [Accessed 2 Feb. 2019].

LoDolce, A. (2019). *Starting a YouTube Channel: ONE thing you MUST do - Viewership Media.* [online] Viewership Media. Available at: https://viewership.com/starting-a-youtube-channel/ [Accessed 2 Feb. 2019].

MakeUseOf. (2019). *7 Things to Consider When Starting a YouTube Channel.* [online] Available at: https://www.makeuseof.com/tag/successful-youtube-channel/ [Accessed 2 Feb. 2019].

Popsci.com. (2019). *Consent Form | Popular Science.* [online] Available at: https://www.popsci.com/learn-new-skills-from-youtube#page-9 [Accessed 2 Feb. 2019].

Quick Sprout. (2019). *7 Hard Hitting Ways to Grow Your YouTube Audience*. [online] Available at: https://www.quicksprout.com/2012/07/23/7-hard-hitting-ways-to-grow-your-youtube-audience/ [Accessed 2 Feb. 2019].

Smarty, A., Moore, J., Smarty, A. and Kakkar, D. (2019). *Back to Basics: 7 Steps for YouTube Success - Search Engine Watch*. [online] Search Engine Watch. Available at: https://searchenginewatch.com/sew/how-to/2232051/back-to-basics-7-steps-for-youtube-success [Accessed 2 Feb. 2019].

Think with Google. (2019). *Self-directed learning from YouTube - Think with Google*. [online] Available at: https://www.thinkwithgoogle.com/advertising-channels/video/self-directed-learning-youtube/ [Accessed 2 Feb. 2019].

Tubular Insights. (2019). *10 Steps to Create an Educational Channel on YouTube: EDU*

Playbook for Teachers. [online] Available at: https://tubularinsights.com/edu-playbook/ [Accessed 2 Feb. 2019].

Winkler, K., Winkler, K. and Winkler, K. (2019). *3 Easy Tools to Create Educational YouTube Videos*. [online] Fractus Learning. Available at: https://www.fractuslearning.com/tools-create-educational-videos/ [Accessed 2 Feb. 2019].

Zimmerman, W. (2019). [online] Workology. Available at: https://workology.com/the-basics-of-starting-a-youtube-channel/ [Accessed 2 Feb. 2019].

3Play Media. (2019). *9 Tips for Your YouTube SEO Strategy – 3Play Media*. [online] Available at: https://www.3playmedia.com/2018/12/20/9-quick-tips-for-youtube-seo-strategy/ [Accessed 2 Feb. 2019].

AdLeaks. (2019). *The Benefits of Using Facebook to Grow a YouTube Channel - AdLeaks*. [online] Available at: https://www.adleaks.com/benefits-using-facebook-grow-youtube-channel/

[Accessed 2 Feb. 2019].

Backlinko. (2019). *YouTube SEO: How to Rank YouTube Videos in 2019*. [online] Available at: https://backlinko.com/how-to-rank-youtube-videos [Accessed 2 Feb. 2019].

Banfield, J. (2019). *Best Practices: Facebook Ads for YouTube Videos*. [online] Jerrybanfield.com. Available at: https://jerrybanfield.com/facebook-ads-for-youtube-videos/ [Accessed 2 Feb. 2019].

Bizwebjournal. (2019). *The 11 Best Ways to Promote Your YouTube Channel – Bizwebjournal*. [online] Available at: https://bizwebjournal.com/promote-youtube-channel/ [Accessed 2 Feb. 2019].

Castillo, M. (2019). *Facebook takes on YouTube with more video advertising options*. [online] CNBC. Available at: https://www.cnbc.com/2018/09/27/facebook-takes-on-youtube-with-more-video-advertising-options.html [Accessed 2 Feb. 2019].

Cheirogergou, K. (2019). *How To 10x Your YouTube Channel Growth In 9 Simple Steps*. [online] Jeffbullas's Blog. Available at: https://www.jeffbullas.com/youtube-channel-growth/ [Accessed 2 Feb. 2019].

fuze. (2019). *3 "Youtube SEO" Basics That Every Marketer Needs To Know - Fuze SEO, Inc..* [online] Available at: http://fuzeseo.co/3-youtube-seo-basics-every-marketer-needs-know/ [Accessed 2 Feb. 2019].

Learn. (2019). *9 proven strategies for promoting your YouTube channel – Learn.* [online] Available at: https://www.canva.com/learn/9-strategies-for-promoting-your-youtube-channel-and-videos-on-social-media/ [Accessed 2 Feb. 2019].

Moz. (2019). *A Step-by-Step Guide to Setting Up and Growing Your YouTube Presence.* [online] Available at: https://moz.com/blog/growing-your-youtube-presence-guide [Accessed 2 Feb. 2019].

Neil Patel. (2019). *A Deep Dive Into Facebook Advertising - Learn How To Make It Work For Your Business!*. [online] Available at: https://neilpatel.com/blog/deep-dive-facebook-advertising/ [Accessed 2 Feb. 2019].

Rich, J. (2019). *Using Instagram to Promote Your YouTube Videos*. [online] Entrepreneur. Available at: https://www.entrepreneur.com/article/310209 [Accessed 2 Feb. 2019].

Si, S. (2019). *The Ultimate Youtube SEO Guide*. [online] Basic and Advanced SEO Tutorials and News - SEO Hacker Blog. Available at: https://seo-hacker.com/youtube-seo/ [Accessed 2 Feb. 2019].

Smarty, A., Moore, J., Smarty, A. and Kakkar, D. (2019). *5 Advanced YouTube SEO Tactics to Drive More Traffic to Your Videos & Website - Search Engine Watch*. [online] Search Engine Watch. Available at: https://searchenginewatch.com/sew/how-to/2340726/5-advanced-youtube-seo-tactics-to-drive-more-traffic-to-your-videos-website [Accessed 2 Feb. 2019].

Wordtracker.com. (2019). *How to optimize your videos for YouTube | Wordtracker.* [online] Available at: https://www.wordtracker.com/academy/marketing/video/seo-basics-for-youtube-videos [Accessed 2 Feb. 2019].

Agrawal, H. (2019). *20 Smart Ways To Get More Subscribers on YouTube in 2019.* [online] ShoutMeLoud. Available at: https://www.shoutmeloud.com/get-youtube-subscribers.html [Accessed 2 Feb. 2019].

Blog.rankingbyseo.com. (2019). [online] Available at: https://blog.rankingbyseo.com/how-to-promote-youtube-videos/ [Accessed 2 Feb. 2019].

Business Insider. (2019). *How To Become The Next YouTube Star Making $100,000 Plus Per Year.* [online] Available at:

https://www.businessinsider.com/how-to-make-money-on-youtube-2010-8#note-youtube-will-only-pay-you-once-your-video-makes-100-11 [Accessed 2 Feb. 2019].

Content Career. (2019). *How To Promote Your YouTube Channel On Instagram - Content Career.* [online] Available at: http://contentcareer.com/blog/how-to-promote-your-youtube-channel-on-instagram/ [Accessed 2 Feb. 2019].

Fullscreen. (2019). *4 ways to grow your YouTube audience with Instagram.* [online] Available at: https://fullscreenmedia.co/2014/07/30/4-ways-grow-youtube-audience-instagram/ [Accessed 2 Feb. 2019].

Hacker Noon. (2019). *6 Additional Ways to Monetize YouTube Videos in 2019.* [online] Available at: https://hackernoon.com/6-additional-ways-to-monetize-youtube-videos-in-2019-160fac9c4d3e [Accessed 2 Feb. 2019].

Insights, C., Guides, V., Vlogging, S., Guide, V., Vlog, H., Channel, G., Views, G., Money, M., Community, B., Sponsorships, Y., Vlogging, B., Resources, C. and Events, I. (2019). *7 Instagram Marketing Tips for Your YouTube Channel | Vlog Nation*. [online] Vlog Nation. Available at: https://www.vlognation.com/instagram-marketing-tips-youtube-channel/ [Accessed 2 Feb. 2019].

Newlands, M. (2019). *How to Get Famous and Make Money On YouTube*. [online] Entrepreneur. Available at: https://www.entrepreneur.com/article/300821 [Accessed 2 Feb. 2019].

Promolta Blog. (2019). *How To Promote Your YouTube Channel Through Instagram Stories - Promolta Blog*. [online] Available at: https://blog.promolta.com/how-to-promote-your-youtube-channel-through-instagram-stories/ [Accessed 2 Feb. 2019].

ReelnReel. (2019). *Ways to Use Instagram to*

Promote YouTube Videos. [online] Available at: https://www.reelnreel.com/ways-use-instagram-promote-youtube-videos/ [Accessed 2 Feb. 2019].

Schneider, B. (2019). *7 Ways to Monetize a Successful Youtube Channel - Resource*. [online] Resource. Available at: http://resourcemagonline.com/2018/09/7-ways-to-monetize-a-successful-youtube-channel/92923/ [Accessed 2 Feb. 2019].

Shane, D. (2019). *5 Reasons Why YouTube May Be Social Media's Greatest Success Story - Social Media Explorer*. [online] Social Media Explorer. Available at: https://socialmediaexplorer.com/content-sections/cases-and-causes/5-reasons-youtube-may-social-medias-greatest-success-story/ [Accessed 2 Feb. 2019].

Snider, S. (2019). *How to Make Money on YouTube*. [online] U.S. News. Available at: https://money.usnews.com/money/personal-finance/family-finance/articles/2018-09-25/how-to-make-money-on-youtube [Accessed 2 Feb. 2019].

StudioBinder. (2019). *How to Start Making Money on YouTube*. [online] Available at: https://www.studiobinder.com/blog/how-to-make-money-on-youtube-video-monetization/#chapter-1 [Accessed 2 Feb. 2019].

Tips, M. (2019). *9 High-Efficiency Ways to Make Money on YouTube in 2019 (Tutorial Guide)*. [online] MiniTool. Available at: https://www.minitool.com/moviemaker/make-money-on-youtube.html [Accessed 2 Feb. 2019].

Shapiro, S. (2019). *What the Future of YouTube Could Look Like*. [online] Observer. Available at: https://observer.com/2015/11/what-the-future-of-youtube-could-look-like/ [Accessed 2 Feb. 2019].

Lightning Source UK Ltd.
Milton Keynes UK
UKHW011900170320
360496UK00001B/55